Reflections
(From a Family Member's Perspective)

Love is surely exemplified in "My Poor Baby," a self-proclaimed love story of Peter and the author, Eugenia Daniels. "My Poor Baby" walks you through the lives of two people who have an appointment with fate because it is love at first sight. This love story will warm hearts and bring smiles on the faces of the reader as the author reminisces about her family's reactions toward her new found beau. Although providence would have them to go in separate directions, explore careers from afar, and find love elsewhere, God's divine intervention would once again intervene decades later. The strong bond of love that was once shared years before is ignited again. However, their lives together the second time around, though short-lived, are even better because of their love for the Lord.

It is amazing to see how God orchestrated the author's career path as a Certified Counselor. He knew beforehand that she would need to be equipped to handle what was to come, even if she did not know right away (Jeremiah 29:11).

This love story would cause tears to form as Daniels describes the pangs of Peter's encounter with the disease of dementia and how people who have this ugly medical condition are treated. We are appreciative of the information she shares about the disease as she speaks candidly about the journey of her "poor baby" and how she tries to give dignity to his life in the midst of it all.

Take a seat. Enjoy this easy reading and enter Peter's world; you too will walk away with a better appreciation of this love story.

Rev. Drs. R. L. & Theresa Holmes
African Methodist Episcopal Church

My Poor Baby

My Poor Baby

Eugenia B. Daniels

Kingdom Living Publishing
Fort Washington, MD

Cover design by TLH Designs, Chicago, IL (www.tlhdesigns.com)

Published by:

Kingdom Living Publishing
Fort Washington, MD 20744
www.kingdomlivingbooks.com

ISBN 978-0-9799798-6-6

Printed in the United States of America

For Worldwide Distribution

Dedication

This book is dedicated to my mother, Ida Dorothy Dudley, who loved my writing and always encouraged me to write. She said my writing depicts my serious and dedicated nature. It also reflects my humorous side that I got from Ma Ment, her mother, Minnie Best. My mother was such a benign person and so extraordinarily faithful to her personal commitment to the service of others. I adored her and it would be an honor for me to be able to carry myself in such a way that it personifies the very essence of her being. I not only want to look just like her, but I want to promulgate the legacy that was the embodiment of a loving, caring, and ingratiating mother.

Acknowledgments

I love my sister, Thelma, and two of my close friends, Jean and Sylvia, more than they will ever know. It is not possible for me to properly reward them for the encouragement they gave me. They kept boosting me on as I tackled thought by thought, impression after impression, and chapter by chapter in an effort to accomplish my dream of completing my first manuscript. You're in my heart guys as I forge ahead embracing one of the most important accomplishments of my life.

Table of Contents

I. Reminiscing

II. Now that We're Together

III. Reflecting and Projecting

Preface

This stage of my life was predestinated and I can see how the threads of my teenage life have connected to the fragments of my adult life. Finally, here I am having lived through the three scores and am now working on the promised ten. I actually feel as if I am going through birth pains and am striving to bring forth a child. From childhood to adulthood, it is impossible to fathom our future. We suffer and agonize over life. Lord, help me to birth this child.

I have come to realize that life is not all about me. There is greater fulfillment in reaching out to help others. There is greater love when shared with others. I have learned to esteem others more than I esteem myself, because in doing so, I reap rewards and gratification that words fail to describe. I know the meaning of the song *"If I Can Help Somebody, Then My Living Will Not Be in Vain."*

I know that a lot has been revealed, but when I think about how what I've shared will help somebody that's in a similar situation, then I know that it will have been well worth my time. As I look out over the Great Smoky Mountains of North Carolina, the foliage is beautiful this time of the year. All of the leaves—and how colorful they are—simply remind me of the people that I hope to help with my memoirs. Truly, this great scenery with the different kind of trees represents all of the cultures, races, and ethnic backgrounds that I hope to reach with my story. There is a compelling drive in us all that transcends particular individuals, specific groups, or renowned communities.

I know that the way of man is not in himself: it is not in man to direct his own steps (Jeremiah 10:23). I know that *the steps of a good man are ordered by the Lord and He delighteth in his way* (Psalm 37:23).

So, I am joyful about my book, believing that the preparations of my heart for the story and the stroke of my pen to write the book were all driven by this inner desire to bring light to the hidden and strength to the yielded.

Foreword

The roads of life are filled with unusual crooks and turns. When the journey begins, there is the tendency to think we are going the right way. The sight of hurt, disappointment, frustration, disgust, embarrassment, jubilation and just pure ecstasy is to far up the road to see clearly.

Tomorrows are not promised to anyone, but trust in the all seeing and all knowing God gives an assurance that all things are working together for the good of them who love Him and are called according to His purpose.

Life does come at us very fast. Despite our plans, whether they include education, marriage, jobs or children, life and time do not wait. Sometimes it seems so unfair as to how things work out, yet we must go on. Somewhere down the road, there is a turn of events that causes one to reflect upon something out of the past. God is so faithful.

This book is written from a real life experience. It is full of details that depict the kinds of unusual turns of events during a span of life. It is refreshing to hear of a spirit of gentleness resulting in the care of a loved one whose health began to deteriorate. This was the personification of the Scripture, 1 Corinthians 13:4-7:

Charity suffereth long, and is kind; charity envieth not; charity vaunteth not itself, is not puffed up, doth not behave itself unseemly, seeketh not her own, is not easily provoked, thinketh no evil; rejoiceth not in iniquity, but rejoiceth in the truth; beareth all things, believeth all things, hopeth all things, endureth all things.

I extend congratulations to a woman whose heart is toward God and His people. It is so real….

The Rt. Reverend Harry L. Cohen
Vice President of the
Southern District Convocation
of the United Holy Church of America, Inc.

I.

Reminiscing

Introduction

Fascination! Fascination! Fascination! What else could a young girl feel when she sees this good looking, curly haired young man walking up to her door smiling from ear to ear greeting her and not asking for her big sister, Litha. I was trying to figure out what he wanted because I knew that I wasn't "taking company" yet. My grandmother had a rule and we knew exactly what it meant when it included courtship. When boys could carry your books home from school and then come back later, that was called courting. I knew that boy could not be coming to talk about schoolwork because I had not seen him at school. I had seen him in the community with my oldest sister's boyfriend.

Well, that contact was the beginning of a lifelong relationship. He was to become my knight in shining armor. We fell deeply in love and thought nothing could separate us. It was as if we were in a world of our own. It was fun and playful.

Join me as I take you on this romantic excursion to learn about love. You'll find out how wonderful it can be and how different it can be.

Love can be so joyful and yet so painful. Love can be so satisfying and somehow unsettling. Love can be so sweet and still so excruciating. Love can seem so warm, but then freeze you to the bone. Love can be so understanding, yet leave you feeling crazy. Love can see one thing, yet your spirit sees something else. Love can be mind boggling, but somehow you're at peace. Love can tear your heart asunder, yet you are able to hold on to your sanity. Love will pull you down in a pit, yet you come out walking on water.

Love, love, love. . . .

We must love. We've got to love. It is the nature of man to love. We have not lived until we have loved—putting ourselves in the plight of others, exposing ourselves to the unpredictable behaviors of others, putting ourselves out there to be embraced, kicked around, or hurt. You have to experience love. It embodies the wows, foes, and ecstasies of life. It is the very essence of our being; and we have not discovered who we are until we have loved.

Chapter One

Doll Baby

During a typical evening in the middle of summer, a young damsel unknowingly caught the eyes of a promising beau. In the midst of a Southern night, scorching heat parched plants but did little to stop the children frolicking down the street. The wisp of a summer's breeze cooled the flesh of teens wooing each other. Folks sitting on their porches waved to cars racing by blowing their horns. Everybody played games and had fun. This was the beginning of a blissful, loving and warm relationship.

I remember those nights as well as I remember my name. I have such loving memories of my teenage years. That's when Peter first saw me. I was just fifteen years old, and he was visiting his girlfriend, who lived next door to my mother. I'd never had any contact with his girlfriend, but I can imagine him clumsily stumbling into her front door while he was looking at me. I was glad that my velvet skin and beauty caught his eye. Even though he did not know how old I was—let alone my name—he decided to find out. Later, he inquired of a mutual friend. He said he wanted to find out who the pretty black girl was who was looking like a little doll baby.

After he found out, Peter came to visit. It was in the afternoon; and my sister Minnie—whom I called Ment—and I were sitting on the porch chatting. He pulled up in a brand new, blue and white Chevrolet Impala.

Ment let out a low whistle. I could not help but smile. Who was this fellow? Not many strangers dropped by our house. He was well dressed, looked like he stepped off the cover of Jet Magazine. My head swayed backward as I took a deep breath engulfing the smell of Old Spice Cologne as he approached the porch.

"Hi, my name's Peter." He extended his hand toward me. "And you're Eugenia."

I put my hand in his, and he pressed a kiss against my skin right on the dimple in my cheek. "Everyone calls me Toni," I said as I blushed, grinning and cutting my eyes at Ment.

My little, short grandmother hurried to the door to see what was happening.

Ma Ment asked, "You here to see Litha?"

Litha was my oldest sister. She already had several prospects, so why couldn't I have this one? I searched Ma Ment's face, trying to get a feel for what she was thinking. We both wondered what would happen next.

Ma Ment said, "Well, son, you didn't answer my question."

He said, "I'm here to see Toni."

She said, "Who are you?"

He replied, "Peter Daniels."

She asked, "Are you from these parts? I've never seen you before."

He said, "Yes mam, I live right around the corner from here on Bright Street."

Ma Ment replied, "You seem to be a nice young man, but Toni isn't allowed to date until she's sixteen. Until then, you can't keep company with her."

The ironic thing about this was how nice he was to my grandmother, after being told that he had to leave. He gave me a wink and a big smile as he walked off the porch.

We ran into the house and Ma Ment was very complimentary about his manners.

She said, "I don't know him but he didn't get agitated by my questions. He spoke well. He answered everything I asked him. He had a pleasant spirit about him." She said he had a good upbringing.

She turned to me and asked, "Toni, how do you know him?"

I replied, "I'd seen him in the neighborhood."

She said, "Do you know his folk?"

I said, "No mam."

I told my grandmother, I may not know him but this one thing I do know, he is another Clark Gable…he is definitely good looking. She smiled. I was surprised that she did not ask him how old he was. Actually, I was glad, because she would have changed her mind about his coming over.

If only the rest of the family had stayed out of it, things would've been fine. I still don't know how Aunt Sissy got so much information or who told her that he was six years older than me. She of course went straight to my mother, who forbade me to see him. They acted like it was a huge age difference. At least Ma Ment didn't think it was so bad.

Peter would stop by when he saw Ma Ment sitting on the porch, so that he could just talk to her. He kept passing by in his car, and I would see him. He didn't stop to talk to me until I turned sixteen. He told Ma Ment that he loved me at first sight and that he wanted to marry me. He kept telling her that and never stopped saying it. I was always curious about what they talked about.

I asked, "Ma Ment, how did you really feel about him?"

"I liked him because I hadn't seen him sneaking around. I feel what he said he really meant. That showed honesty in his character. That's good."

That seemed to be the longest year of my life. I never knew exactly when he would drive by. I was elated when I would catch a glimpse of him riding by in that bad car. I could just picture myself riding in the front seat next to him. I could picture us riding so closely that it just looked like one person was in the car.

During that year as he was waiting for me to celebrate my sixteenth birthday, he got drafted into the Army. That was in my freshman year. What a drag. What a bomb. Uncle Sam just snatched my beau from me.

Peter came home as often as he could. We couldn't go out too often even though I was in the tenth grade. So, we mostly watched television, the Ed Sullivan Show and went to the movies. He was so sweet and generous. Even though I was young and innocent, I never had a problem eating in front of him. I talked to my girlfriends who said they got choked up trying to eat in front of boys. I always ate. I loved the fifteen cent hot dogs. He would order me one "all the way," which meant I would have mustard, ketchup, onions, chili, and slaw. I'd drink a Root Beer soda or a Sun Crest orange soda. We'd go to a little "drive up" shack on the corner of Elm and George Streets. We called this eating out.

Peter would say, "You good?"

I'd reply, "Yep."

He gave me gifts at Christmas and on my birthday. I'll always remember the year that he bought me a Bulova watch.

We wrote so many letters and sent so many cards—my niece would tell me forty years later that she still saw cards and letters in the home place with his name on them.

I fell in love with him, and told him that I would marry him after high school. I fell in love with him because he was so gentle. I looked forward to the times we spent together.

Being in Peter's arms was soft like a pillar of clouds. His touch was comforting and mesmerizing.

His love was so heartwarming. I felt so protected that it could be compared to handling fine china. I felt I would not be hurt or broken. We were so in love and having so much fun together.

The one person that I didn't want to know about our relationship actually found out that I was seeing Peter. I know that it was my Aunt Sissy who finally disclosed my secret to my mother. I really couldn't say anything to my Aunt Sissy because we didn't talk back to grown folk. I didn't like it one bit. I was so mad with her because this was none of her business. In a strange way, I felt she thought she was being helpful. Her motives didn't surprise me; Aunt Sissy didn't play. There was no smoking in our home, and drinking was out of the question.

We were raised in a Christian home. My great grandmother was a preacher and so was her daughter, Aunt Sissy. The music in the world was the devil's music. They called that kind of music "reals," and we weren't supposed to play it in our home.

We had a wholesome childhood; and Mother made sure that we were exposed to cultural things such as learning to play the piano. We all took music lessons but nobody played. I was pretty good, but we all stopped taking lessons because nobody else in the neighborhood was taking lessons.

When Aunt Sissy was not at home after school, I would call my singing group, and they'd come over. The piano would be rocking, and we would be singing our little hearts out. We had someone on the lookout for my aunty, just in case she came home early. We'd be practicing, playing reels and singing those devil songs. My Aunt Sissy was in what they called the "prayer band," and they'd visit the sick and shut-in members to pray with them. While she was gone, we'd just be having a ball. But, when we got the cue, everyone would scramble out of the house. By the time my aunt got home, we'd be in our room doing homework. Sometimes, we'd put on gospel music and be looking so innocent.

After Aunt Sissy ratted me out to my mother, I took to calling her Snoopy. I'd get a whipping every time my mom would find out that I'd seen Peter. Snoopy enjoyed telling her everything. She even got into our conversations on the telephone. I'm used to three-way calls. Snoopy invented them way back in the day.

I really wanted to marry Peter until it was time. Then I started to think about college more and more. Maybe I was too young to get married and to have a family. There was no doubt that he'd be a good husband. My grandmother was very pleased with him and the way he was treating me. It was just that I became quite career oriented and decided not to be swept away into holy matrimony at age eighteen.

During my senior year in high school, Peter was discharged from the Army, and I informed him of my decision.

I said, "I know I promised to get married Peter, but I want to go to college."

"Marry me and let me send you to college."

I responded, "What if I get pregnant? School will be out."

"I promise you an education. We'll work it out. You'll see."

I could see the hurt in his eyes. I could feel the hurt in his heart as he kept trying to convince me that he would make good on his word. He stood up, went to the door, and looked around at me as I sat on the sofa.

"Come here," he murmured.

"What was it that made you doubt me?"

"Toni," he said, "you know how much I love you. Now that I can finally have you for myself as my wife to take care of you. . ., this is what you tell me."

"Why?"

He held me so tightly. I felt the pain and starting crying. He looked right into my eyes and said,

"I'm going to White Plains. I'll give you time to reconsider. I can't take it. I'm leaving."

Chapter Two

Agonizing Enlightenment

Leaving high school and going to college, what a change. I left most of my friends from elementary school through high school to go to Fayetteville State University. It was strange not having the twins in class. There'd been three sets of twins in my class for as long as I could remember--twin girls, twin boys, and a set with a girl and boy. I spent many hours flipping through the pages of my high school yearbook.

While the transition was quite smooth, I longed for my beloved. I missed his broad smile and warmth. I agonized over his prolonged absence from my life although it was my decision. Notwithstanding, I resigned myself to pursue the awesome task before me with all of my being. I was embarking upon an educational goal that would lead to a promising career, which would culminate into a successful profession.

Peter wrote letters letting me know that he missed me and hoped that I would change my mind. I wrote back letting him know that the feeling was mutual but I still felt I wanted my education first.

He returned home a few months after I left for college. He knew by my actions that I was serious about college. I didn't hear from him very much after that. I only came home three times a year: Thanksgiving, Christmas, and Easter. Other than that, I stayed at school until summer.

Visiting me at school was simply out of the question, because we had to be in our dorms by 7:00 p.m. every night. From 7:00 p.m. until 9:00 p.m., we had study hall. We could study in the specified study areas in the dorm—our own dorm not someone else's—or we could go to the library on campus.

On the weekends, the only way that we could go anywhere was by written permission from our parents. Now, we could go downtown shopping. If we went to the movies, we had to sit upstairs. Those were still Jim Crow days. The movie to see back then was "The Liberation of L. B. Jones." That movie ruined the careers of some of the actors. At least that's what I've always believed. I was totally engulfed with new, amazingly enlightening endeavors.

We picketed lunch counters and movies back then. Large groups of us gathered together and marched downtown with our signs. I made a sign that read "We Shall Overcome. . ." I remember one of my other signs that read "We Are Equal." I felt a sense of pride that enabled me to withstand verbal abuse and even being spit on. Retaliation never entered my mind or spirit. I took it like a bold soldier in the Army. I was conditioned for the marches because my pastor at home had led us through the streets of Goldsboro. We marched from Big Ditch Church on Elm Street to Center Street in the downtown area.

There was so much going on during my freshman year, I really didn't have time for dating. To make a really long story short, Peter and I drifted apart. He was carrying on his life, and I was busy in college pursuing my education. I marvel at my tenacity even today. Why did I allow that bridge to crumble?

Chapter Three

Jumping over the Broom

Where's the broom, Toni? The question remained even after I finished college. When was I going to get married? I was full of knowledge and energy. I had fresh ideas and oddly enough—none of them envisioned the almighty jump over the broom at that moment in time. With all of the new things that I'd learned and with a different outlook on life, I raced to conquer the myriad of challenges I faced.

I eliminated obstacle after obstacle that would hinder my progress. I was fortunate to be hired for a teaching position after only one job interview. I really counted that as a blessing from God. A large number of my fellow cohorts went out of state for employment. I wanted to stay in North Carolina for my first two years. Then, I wanted to travel with my girlfriends, finding teaching jobs in various states for a period of ten years. Afterwards, we'd settle down and get married—provided Mr. Right came along.

Upon graduating from college, my girlfriends and I worked in Kinston, North Carolina. I worked there for three years and they worked two years. I taught Business Education classes at Adkin Senior High School.

We bought cars. Monique bought a brand new Malibu. I bought a used 1962 burgundy Bonneville. My other friend was Johnquil. I cannot remember the kind of car she drove. Back then recaps had just hit the market. I rode them and kept extras in the trunk. Monique would buy new tires. Recapped tires were only ten dollars apiece. A whole set of tires were only forty dollars and they lasted a long time-- just about three to six months. If a lot of highway driving were done, the rubber would peel off and the car would start chugging alone making loud noises. I bought recaps so that I could spend my money on clothes.

We all spent lots of money on new clothes and kept up with the latest fashion. Everytime we stepped out to a party or to the club, we would be the "show stoppers." We had on our little "a line" dresses and matching scarves with matching shoes and pocketbooks. We enjoyed single life. It felt great to be independent. I was proud to show my family what I could do by myself.

Well, after a couple of years of living it up, I began to think about someone I'd met while in college. I worked on campus in the Alumni Relations Office. Suddenly one day, I looked away from the paper I was typing. Wow, I thought. Who was that young man and what was the nature of his business?

He said, "Hi."

I replied, "Hello. If you're looking for Mr. Maynard, my boss, he's not in."

He said, "My name is Raymone and I'm here to see you. Your name is Toni."

I said, "Yes, but" and he interrupted me saying that he found out who I was after seeing me walk across the campus a couple of days ago. He was with a buddy who was visiting his girlfriend. The girlfriend gave him my name and where I worked.

Raymone told me that he fell in love with me the moment he saw me. He thought that I was the most beautiful girl that he had ever seen. I thought to myself: "He's a soldier and probably well traveled." He kept talking. He told me that the moment he saw me, he said, "That's my wife."

Instant love! Love at first sight! That was all that he could imagine and that was what he kept saying.

So, now that I had taught for a couple of years, I really started thinking about that broom.

We fell in love and got married. So, I jumped the broom with someone besides Peter. We had a great life together for sixteen of the twenty-two years that we were married. We traveled overseas to Germany, where he was stationed in Hanau.

I loved Europe. I worked there in the Army Education Center as an Education Specialist. I had to commute to Buedingen, which was about thirty kilometers away from the military caserne where we lived. I had a little Volkswagen Bug, navy blue. It took me about forty-five minutes to get to work each morning. Sometimes, I would arrive on post just as the soldiers were in formation getting their morning briefing from the commanding officer.

It would be so embarrassing to have to walk where all of those men would be looking at me. The style was hip huggers, miniskirts, and clogs. I knew how soldiers were; and I knew that they would have a hay day if something unusual were to happen as I passed by them. I felt as if I was looking really cute on that day. I worried about misstepping in my clogs because I was a little nervous. I could hear the comments they'd make if I fell off of my shoes.

One morning, I was walking and stepped on a small rock. I didn't know anyone was watching, but I'm sure that whoever was watching got a good laugh. It took me a minute to regain my composure. I straightened up, fixed my coat, pushed my shoulders back, stuck my head in the air, and kept right on stepping.

I went to Spain, Holland, and England. I actually saw a bull fight in Barcelona. I learned to snow ski in the Alps. I bought a clock, bone China, and clothes. I had enough outfits to fill three closets.

Yes, I was moving on with my life, but so was Peter. He jumped over the broom before I did. He married a young lady from Goldsboro named Amy Farland a few months after I left for college. They moved to New Jersey and had four lovely children, two girls and two boys. The years just zipped right on by as we lived our lives apart from each other.

Chapter Four

The Green Giant

I divorced in February 1991, and Peter's wife passed in April of the same year. Three years later, during the Christmas holidays, he came looking for me. He was quite persistent, because no one was giving him any information about me. I'd put the word out to my family that I didn't want to be contacted by anybody, and I didn't care who it was. I had come home to rest and relax with my family. I even stayed with one of my sisters to ensure that I would not be disturbed. One night at Ment's, the door bell rang. I told her to get the door, because I knew that it couldn't be anyone for me. Ment came to the back and insisted that I go answer it.

I asked, "Who is it?"

"Peter."

I got an attitude. I put both hands on my hips and just stomped on the floor in disgust. I did open the door but I just stood there. I was determined not to invite him in because I'd made up my mind that I would spend the time with my sister. We stood in the door and he just kept on talking and talking. Finally, he asked if he could come in.

I stepped back and let him in. He started talking about his brand new 1994 Cadillac and how he had paid cash for it. He referred to his Caddy as "The Green Giant." He asked if I wanted to see it, and I told him no thank you. I noticed that he kept starring at me. He was looking me over from head to toe.

It aroused my curiosity, so I asked, "Why are you scoping me out so carefully?"

He said, "I haven't seen you in such a long time. Can't I look at you?"

Later, months later, he admitted that he was comparing the "new" Toni with the "old" one, summing up the difference. He told me that the jean dress I'd worn was too big. Not only that, but the dress was ugly, and my slip had been hanging out. He was wondering what had happened to that cute little doll baby he'd known. He told me that my hair needed to be combed.

I mean he poured it on, and all I could do was laugh. Truly, I hadn't been out trying to catch anyone. I'd really had on one of Ment's old dresses and could have cared less about how I looked. He did say that I still had that velvet skin and that my face was as pretty as ever. My impression of him was that he was just as good looking as ever. I did not need to be seeing him. It would be like playing with fire--anything that hot would burn.

I told Peter the reason I did not ask him in was because dating was not an interest of mine. I told him that I was not trying to be rude. I gave my life to Christ in 1988 and had not dated since. I wanted to live for the Lord and dating could lead to unforeseen troubles. Everything I stood for could be lost just for a moment of passion. I didn't want to live that way. Jesus was all that I needed.

He insisted on taking me out to dinner and kept saying how harmless that would be. He promised not to try to kiss me. He was persistent, but I had stamina and stayed my course, immovable. He talked for another hour.

Ment and Don (another sister) just kept prancing through the living room going to the kitchen for water. They were looking at me, making faces as they went through. They were excited because someone had come to see their "saved" sister. I hadn't dated in six years. It was no wonder they were beside themselves.

When Peter finally left, they almost knocked me down getting to the window to see that brand new Caddy.

"Come on, girl. You know you want to see that car," Don called.

"No, I don't." But I dashed to the window to look at it. My, my, my, what a fantastic ride.

My sisters knew that I didn't date. I was not about to compromise my relationship with Jesus. I was serious about my walk with God, and I didn't accept dinner dates, movie dates, or any other dates. I knew that would not be the end of it. I wanted to really live holy and not straddle the fence. I knew people who had a "top of the mountain" testimony on Sunday mornings, but lived a "down in the valley" lifestyle

Monday through Friday. They lived one day a week for the Lord and six days a week for the devil.

I wanted to live a life that was dedicated, committed, and consistent with the Word of God. My life had to be congruent and balanced, and I knew that it was possible because of the Holy Spirit living within me.

I called my mother's house later that night and demanded to know who had sniffed me out.

My big brother, Leamon, Jr., got on the phone and said, "I gave the boy the address and told him how to get there. Anybody who comes somewhere eight or nine times looking for someone, I'm gonna tell 'em. Yeah, I told it. I would want someone to do the same for me. I felt sorry for the brother."

All I could do was laugh. My brother was crazy.

Don and Ment tried to convince me to at least go on one date. I told them all I got out of that night was a good testimony. When I got back to church after the holidays, I told about the experience. In the Fire Baptized movement, there were twelve nights of consecration services at the beginning of each New Year. I could hardly wait to give my testimony. When the time came for devotional leaders to take their position, I almost ran to the front of the church.

I told the saints how the devil was on the job. One can't run or hide when he's on your trail because he'll sift you out. I told them how I was minding my own business, trying to live righteous and holy for the Lord, when the devil showed up in a green, spanking brand new Cadillac that he'd paid cash for. I told that devil that I was saved and I didn't want a ride. Furthermore, I told him that I didn't date because that was the first step to hell. And I didn't want to go there.

I told him that I was through with the things of the world. The devil didn't have anything I wanted or needed, and I surely wasn't going back. I loved the Lord, and there's no devil in hell that would steal my joy or my place in heaven. Oh! I had a testimony. I turned my back on the new car, the handsome driver, and the money. I knew that I was saved. I was tempted, and I didn't give in. I was sought out, but I wasn't bought out. Yeah! Yeah! He went on 'bout his business. After he got out of sight, I couldn't tell which way he went.

Chapter Five

Time Passes. . . Things Change

Six years went by, and one summer night in May, the doorbell rang. I looked at my watch, because to me it was too late for someone to be just stopping by. It was about 9:15 p.m., and I was on the way to bed. Well, at least I had no plans of going out again.

"Who's there?"

"Peter."

"Just a minute." I changed clothes quickly and found myself smiling as I opened the door. "I'm glad to see you. How did you know I was here?"

"I always drive by to see if your car is here anytime I'm in Goldsboro." He looked down at his feet and glanced at me.

Then stated, "Raphael mentioned something about it, too."

That sounded like my brother-in-law. After inviting him in and sitting down, I felt strange. I began to ponder this weird feeling. I was feeling really happy and delighted that he was there. Where was this coming from? We were chatting as if we'd seen each other a day or so ago.

He reached for my hand, and I let him take it. "Will you marry me?"

My mouth flew open. "Why," I asked. "We haven't seen each other in six years, and we haven't been together since I was in high school."

"I want you." His hand trembled as it held mine. He got off the sofa, bent down on one knee, and looked me right in the eyes.

"I want you to be my wife. I'll never forget when I asked you to be my wife. I asked you to marry me when you were a senior in high school, remember?"

"Yes, but that was forty years ago."

"I want you to be mine forever, Toni." His eyes searched mine. "Don't you remember when I told Ma Ment that I loved you and wanted you to be my wife when you were only sixteen years old?"

My heart panted as I pictured him standing at the door when I was a senior in high school. He asked me then.

Now, he's asking me again to marry him.

This time I asked him, "Why?"

Things are complicated with me now because of my Christian beliefs. I felt different and I believed that I needed to seek the Lord for spiritual guidance. I certainly realized that I had experienced a change of heart. I did not understand it. I just knew it in my spirit.

"I have to see what the Lord says about this because I have a living spouse, and my knowledge of the Word is that

I have to stay single. Plus, I can't marry someone who isn't a Christian." The Bible says that Christians cannot be un-equally yoked.

I vowed to seek the face of God, but in the meantime, I did allow him to take me out to dine several times. We even went to the movies to see "The Perfect Storm." I remembered that he was a good kisser. Was he still? Fond memories kept flooding my mind. I also remembered all of the love letters he'd written me while he was still in the Army. I recalled the times when he came home for the holidays. I felt like a teenager again. I was full of life, vim and vigor. Not a care in the world when he was around.

Finally, in September, I fasted and prayed for seven days. I read Scripture after Scripture about marriage and how one lives in adultery, if he remarries while the ex-spouse is still alive. It was toward the end of the fast when I got the revelation of Matthew 5:32. It said divorce was acceptable for one reason and one reason only: fornication with some-one other than your spouse. I didn't know why, but until then, I'd disregarded that Scripture—even when others had brought it to my attention. I recalled having done that on an Upward Bound trip when a bus driver attempted to clarify the Scripture.

I'd always felt that unless you caught the person in the act, you really didn't have a case. Somehow, I felt you had to prove the allegation without a shadow of doubt. But then, who would be dumb enough to get caught? But in the natural sense, a child from a sexual act is undisputable proof of infidelity, especially if the man claimed the child as his.

Well, after having clarity on that issue, it was now time to deal with another one—not being unequally yoked (2 Corinthians 6:14). I told him that Christians are not free to marry non-Christians and wanted to know if he were saved. He asked me how to get saved, which told me the answer was no. I told him one had to ask the Lord to come into his heart and have a sincere mind to change his way of living (John 3:16). One couldn't get saved just because he wanted to marry somebody. I told him that God knows the heart, and if the request for Him to come in wasn't sincere, then God wouldn't honor that request.

I explained the willingness to change one's lifestyle, because it was more than just uttering words. Once the request was made, God would make changes in his life. He told me he wasn't going to church on a regular basis. He had a friend who had been trying to get him to attend his church. That friend was a faithful member of his church and a devout lover of the Lord, as well a worker in the church.

Time passed, and I got a call from Peter. He told me he'd stopped smoking and drinking and was going to church with his friend on a regular basis. He told me when the pastor called folk to the altar for prayer, he went up and told the pastor he wanted to give his life to the Lord. The pastor prayed with him, and Peter gave his life to God. He joined the church and was baptized a few weeks later.

He called me every night wanting to talk about church. He felt so different, and he was glad he'd given his life to Christ. I bought him a New Believer's Bible and sent it to him. I was eager to see him again, so we could attend church together, pray together, and witness the beauty of salvation together. He came to Goldsboro for Thanksgiving, and I noticed a change. There was a calmness of spirit and sheer joy when he talked about not smoking anymore. He told me that if the Lord could free him of his nicotine habit, he considered that a miracle in and of itself. He'd been smoking for over forty years. He was so excited, and it appeared to me that he saw God as a bona fide champion.

God is awesome, able to do anything. There is nothing too hard for Him. His Word tells us that in the book of Isaiah. I loved the way the Lord proved Himself faithful to Peter. Even though Peter had tried to stop smoking on several occasions, it wasn't until he had God's help that he quit.

When I saw him and realized that he'd really changed, I accepted his proposal. I told him that we shouldn't get married in a hurry. We needed to take our time.

"How much longer do I have to wait?" he asked. "It's already been forty years."

I told him that I'd buy a wedding book and start looking through it. I even told him that I would ask my sister, Don, if she would direct the wedding. I did ask my sister, and she was ecstatic about directing the gala affair. She asked me when the wedding bells would ring. I told her that I was in no hurry and that I was going to ask one of his daughters to assist her with the wedding.

I asked his daughter, Patricia, to assist with the wedding, and she agreed after letting me know that this would be a brand new adventure for her. I let her know that my sister was in the same boat.

Peter told me that he wanted to talk to my dad because it was the proper thing to do. I was surprised because as two fully "seasoned" adults, I didn't even think about that. He wanted to ask for my hand in marriage. My dad's blessing meant a lot to Peter. When I told my dad that my knight in shining armor wanted to talk to him, he said to bring him to the Bolton's family reunion at the Boys and Girls Club. As soon as he saw Peter, recognition flashed in his eyes. My father was indeed delighted to discuss the matter and was tickled pink about Peter's demeanor and mannerism. Peter was such a gentleman, and he was so sincere.

Peter returned to New Jersey but had already made it clear that he would definitely return for Christmas. During his absence, he continued to attend church and told me that he was asked to become an usher. He also told me that he would go to Bible Study, but due to working on the grave-yard shift, it wasn't possible. He certainly appeared to have a hunger for the Word. I was pleased and very much impressed. Something else that caught my attention was his verbalization. He had begun to talk more, and he enjoyed conversing about his new life.

Time seemed to pass so swiftly. The Christmas holidays came, and we found ourselves right back in each other's arms again. We engaged in various activities such as going on long drives, seeing movies, shopping at the malls, dining out, and visiting family. We were just having a grand time.

In the meantime, something began to resonate in our minds. We started realizing that it was getting increasingly more difficult to be together and to continue shunning closeness. A couple of days later, we just decided that we would forego all of the pomp and circumstance of a formal wedding and have an intimate ceremony. We set the date, got the license, contacted the minister, and rushed out and bought the rings.

We got married on December 18, 2000. We told our family members the next few days. While some of them resented being left out, others gave us their blessings. In March of the next year, we announced our marriage in the "Goldsboro News Argus." We were two happy little larks.

II.

Now That
We're Together

Chapter Six

Honeymoon Basking

We were so happy and very much in love. We traveled wherever we wanted to go. We immediately started calling each other by the nicknames that we chose. I called him Baby and Big Head, because I'd seen a picture of him when he was about six or seven and he'd had the biggest little head. He called me his "Sunshine," because he said that I had brought so much joy into his life.

He took me to Niagara Falls on our honeymoon. While there, he told me that he was taking me on a second honeymoon to the Bahamas. He made sure that he was doing things right. This was more than cake and ice cream—this treat was eggs over lightly, biscuit and gravy with chips of sausage and a dab of Karo Syrup. This marriage had the workings of a masterful hand.

When we went to the Bahamas, we. . . Well, anyway, we were enjoying our country selves. I must say that on one very special afternoon, we slipped into our swimwear. I tied my beach scarf around my hips and Peter had on his Bahama jamma pants. We proceeded to get into the Jacuzzi near the ocean. The jets were propelling, the water was splashing and hitting all the right places—in our backs and on our thighs.

Lo and behold, we started seeing people approach. It seemed as if these folk were walking right toward us. I cleared my throat and coughed that little cough when things are about to get out of hand. We got frigidity, and apparently, Peter was showing much discomfort. When I looked around at him, he was beet red. We took flight. We weren't used to being in close quarters with strangers, especially while being so sparsely clad. We weren't even used to being in a Jacuzzi with anyone, quite frankly.

We went down to the ocean and got in the water where we were more comfortable.

On numerous occasions, we dined at exquisite restaurants where we ate shrimp as big as butter fish. All of the seafood there was so much larger than back in the States. We had loads of fun on our honeymoon. All I could think about was that after all those years, we were together at last. What was so good about it was that we not only loved one another, we loved Jesus. We were able to share our love in our personal relationship, and on a deeper level, the agape love through Christ. The greatest love of all was the love of Jesus. For with that love, therein lied one's destiny. For with that love, we were empowered to make it through all of life's seasons with abundant joy and success. May get wounded sometimes, but. . . .

We had indeed finished several changing seasons in our lives only to begin what was to be the last and final phase. Neither of us had sixty or seventy years more in this life's space. So, I was determined to stay the course and not falter along the way.

I envisioned our excursion as a cruise on the great oceans of life. Emotions swelled in me. I splashed about on turbulent waters. . .; dashed and thrust to and fro from the fierceness of gigantic waves. Still I forged ahead.

While honeymooning, I'd think about our future, our life together as husband and wife, Mr. and Mrs. Walter Daniels. I thought about how Peter was quick to correct people who would refer to me by my former name. I'd smile because that made me feel special.

Scars and bruises would be present as we made our way through the seasons of life. Those precious thoughts were nestled deep down on the inside of me. I kept nudging and pulling and nudging and pulling at them until they leaped out. . . .

Life's Pondering Moments

Baby, Baby
What is this…
What is this feeling?
You've got me swirling and reeling
And moving about aimlessly.

SHEER WONDERMENT

What are you doing to me?
In zero degree weather
I'm perspiring when I should be shivering
You're not even with me
But I feel you
And you're warmer than my covers
Blissful, enrapturement, aphrodisia
Moments, Moments, Pondering Moments.

UNIMAGINABLE

You're not even with me
But I smell you
I smell you, Baby
In the spring time
I know you're there
You're there.

YOU'RE PEACHY AND SWEET

You chase me through
The strawberry patch.
When I fall down, you pick me up
You lick my lips
My tongue
Slides into your mouth…umph
You kiss me
Leaving that sweet strawberry
Taste in my mouth.
I can taste you.

UNBELIEVABLE

YOU TASTE GOOD
Ummmmph…
WOW, WOW
You're SO GOOD!
When I close my eyes
I see you.

UNDERGIRDING AND COMPASSIONATE

Pulling me up when I'm blue
Bearing my pain in longsuffering,
Smothering me in love and

Holding me close 'til the hurt is gone.
Whispering, "It's gonna be alright Sunshine."
Telling me, "Together, nothing is impossible."

ESSENCE OF LOVE – UNCONQUERABLE

Love is undeniable, all encompassing, delightful
Love is imbalance, undefeatable and mushy
Love is overflowing, inundating
We're basking in it
Submerging ourselves in it
Engulfing ourselves in it
Dousing and plunging.

SATIATING

We can make it 'cause
In us
There's a
LIGHT that SHINES.
We can make it 'cause
In us
There's a
FIRE THAT BURNS.
We can make it 'cause
In us
That LIGHT IS JESUS

In us
That FIRE IS THE HOLY GHOST

THERE IS NONE GREATER – JESUS IS INDOMITABLE!

So, when we left the Bahamas, I knew that we would make it through every season of life because we would hold onto each other and we would cling to God.

Chapter Seven

The Right Place or the Wrong Place

We'd been together for a while now. We were still in love but beginning to notice some little quirks about each other. One day, I was making the bed and moving from side to side in an attempt to get it just right. I tucked the covers under and stepped back to check it out. I went back around to the other side of the bed, looked back at the other side, and felt that I needed to go back over a spot. On the way back, I realized something that had eluded me until then. I kept having to brush pass my husband. I had to skip one time, because I almost stepped on his toes. At another time, I had to make a quick move to avoid backing into him.

I said, "Excuse me."

Well, for some reason he would move, but it would always be in another place that was still in my way. I began to wonder if bending over so much had "a sexual thing" with him, or if he just wanted to have me knocking into him for some kind of contact. All I really knew was that being close that way was getting on my nerves. Couldn't he see that I was trying to make the bed and to finish what I was doing? I wasn't sending any secret messages or codes with my body. I was actually trying to get the bed done, so I could move on to something else for the day. This happened quite a lot. Should I address the issue? No. I didn't have the time to make a long conversation out of every little thing I did around the house. Plus, he was still my Baby.

Another day, some money slipped down the drain in the kitchen. Why? He was taking change in and out of his pocket, and a penny just got away from him. He didn't realize it. I was the one who found the penny in the drain and tried to fetch it. That's when it slipped and went right down the drain. Well, yeah, I wanted to holler out, but I didn't. I just said, "We'll have to get the plumber over soon, because the kitchen sink is stopped up."

He wanted to know what in the world happened. I told him that some money had gotten into the drain. My Baby had no clue how money had actually found its way into the kitchen sink. Then, I mentioned how he loved to play with money, taking it in and out of his pocket. He claimed he didn't even have any pennies, that he only did that with quarters. So, I guess the penny got off the dresser and just came walking into the kitchen.

I called the plumber and told him that a penny was in our kitchen sink and the water was backing up. Later that morning, the plumber came. I missed my husband, but then I heard the plumber say, "Sir, I need to get right there where you are."

Right at the very moment that the plumber arrived, my husband decided he wanted some ice cream. He got the ice cream from the freezer and just stood right in front of the kitchen sink and proceeded to eat his ice cream. He was in the way. He was at the wrong place. Now, to him he was always at the right place at the right time. He had options that most folk would have chosen, which would have been a better place to be at that particular time. Not my Baby, he chose to be in the way.

It wasn't too much later when I reached into the closet to find a change of clothes for the day. I got the outfit I wanted, stepped back, turned around, and whose foot did I step on? Peter was right there in my way. On another occasion, I found myself in a stooped position, looking under the kitchen counter with the cabinet doors open getting a storage dish for leftovers. I got what I wanted, turned to put the dish on the table, and who did I bump into? Peter was right there again—in my way. Yep, that's my Baby always in my way.

Sometimes I worried about this right-place-wrong-place thing. When we finished playing golf at Meadow View Golf Course, we got our bags and headed for the van. Well, I put the key in the lock to open the lift gate, turned around, and Peter wasn't there. I looked around and found him standing behind a car in the midst of some white men, whom he didn't know. The golfers were perplexed; it was quite evident by the look on their faces. I immediately called his name to entice him to leave that area and come to me. I was very uneasy, because not very many blacks played on that course. Had I not been with him, I often think about what might have happened. We had only played there a couple of times. At least during those times, everyone was friendly.

I remembered a time at a Seven-Eleven mart, when my husband had finished pumping gas, he went inside. It seemed as if he would never come out of the store. Although it was very crowded, he should've come out in less than thirty minutes. There were other customers who went in after he did and came out much sooner. During the time I was waiting, I began to notice a young man, who stepped out of the mart and stood by the door looking from side to side, beckoning other young men to come where he was.

All I could do was to sit there picturing my husband taking money in and out of his pocket, spreading it on the counter as he would do on occasion, when paying for merchandise. I believed those young men were tempted by this behavior and were casing the place, trying to get a feel for the right time to mug him. I felt this could have happened, because there were four or five of them and only one of him. It seemed the manager on duty was a woman. I felt so uneasy that I began to plead the blood of Jesus as I was getting out of the car to check on him.

At that very moment, he came out of the store looking quite eerie. I asked him if someone had tried to hurt him in the mart. He told me they hadn't. I asked him if one of those young men said anything to him, and he told me no.

Whatever those young men intended to do at that mart did not go down, because a praying believer spoke the Word. They were stopped in their tracks.

The right-place-wrong-place became an issue in Louisiana. We went to New Orleans, having already been on our second honeymoon, and another very weird incident occurred as we sat in in the airport awaiting our flight home. A man and his wife were starring at Peter and just laughing and picking and poking at him. They would utter words to each other, look at him and start laughing. They got really loud and that drew my attention to them. Puzzled by this craziness, I sneered, stretched my neck forward, made an ugly face, dropped my mouth opened as if to say, "Are you stupid or what? This man is not bothering you. What is your problem?"

They seemed to have gotten worse. After I noticed my husband's demeanor, pensive, shameful, and degrading, we got up to leave, but the agent called our flight number. That ended the charade, but I still found it difficult to believe that people would be so disrespectful in a public place to a total stranger.

Chapter Eight

Loving and Learning

We continued to love one another and to enjoy selected moments together. Because I was still working, I looked forward to coming home—opening the garage door and seeing my Baby standing in the dining room door waiting for his Sunshine. We would be kissing and embracing to the extent that if anyone were to observe us, one would think that I had been gone for a week. I loved how he would take his left arm and pull me to him with that broad smile and his "umm-huh, this is my lady" look.

I'd wiggle out of his arms. . .; sometimes. I had to cook. I enjoyed cooking for Peter. It was such a delight, because he wasn't picky. He enjoyed the hearty meals I prepared and usually ate everything on his plate. My Baby was so sweet. He would wash the dishes after supper, and not because I'd asked him to. He'd just get up, run the water, pour the soap, and do the job.

After dinner, we'd go walking in the backyard. The area stretched the length of a football field. We'd talk about how it might have been had we gotten together years ago. We held hands and the emotions could be felt as we reminisced. On nights when we'd had rain, we'd head over to the track. The gravel was hard on the knees, but we liked it better than squishy shoes. If it were still pouring, we'd go to the mall.

Often our conversation drifted to what we'd done during the day. I always knew what he wanted to know and that was when I would be retiring. He constantly reminded me that I'd promised to retire in 2002. Here it was 2003, and I was still working.

Peter also wanted to go to work with me. I worked in education as a school counselor. I am also an ordained minister. Counseling was my full-time career. There were times when I would take him with me, and he would spend the day with one of my friends who was an auto mechanic. Martell worked on my ministry van and one of my cars. Those were some very select moments that were nice.

One thing I liked about Peter going with me was the relief from driving. I'd commuted to Bladen County for twenty-three years, and it was a joy to have someone else drive occasionally. I tried to take him when I'd have sports events at the school. I'd have to stay late, because I was on duty.

Peter was eager for me to retire. He'd taken the leisure route immediately after we jumped over the broom. He was ready to move down South, and in February, 2001, he retired from his job in New Jersey. We'd packed his things and moved him to Fayetteville a few days later, only to have him head back up for several months. His youngest son, Nathan, broke his arm and was unable to work. Peter remained with Nathan until he was good as new.

I love the fatherly passion he has for his children. It was a spontaneous move. There were no options. I missed him and was happy when he returned.

Peter had looked forward to spending more time with me, so I officially retired in February 2003. I had to return to work due to the sudden death of Kathy, the school counselor who had relieved me. She and her entire family were killed in a private plane crash. I returned and worked until June of that year. This was puzzling to Peter.

He asked, "Why can't they hire another counselor? You just retired. I want you home with me."

"It was not enough time. All counselors were needed to organize grief counseling teams. Kathy had worked in the system and was well known to the students."

The school year finally ended. My husband was so glad to have me home with him that he couldn't stop hugging me. He gave me that broad smile. Quite frankly, I was glad to be home after thirty-two years of service in education and social work. I'd had a very rewarding career and would've worked a few more years had I not gotten married.

Being home started tuning me into things that I'd missed when I was employed. Peter went to the Veterans Administration Hospital (VAH) for regular doctor's appointments concerning shortness of breath and ringing in his ear. The doctor performed a complete physical on Peter's initial visit and gave a diagnosis of hypertension. Peter was given medication for that, along with pills for the ringing in his ear, and a pump for breathing problems.

To stay busy, Peter volunteered at the VAH and worked with the soldiers in the nursing home. He seemed to be doing well. I didn't accompany him to the doctor, but I would inquire about the visit upon his return. I recalled when I was working and would ask him about his visit with the doctor Peter would give me specific details. He could remember the name of his doctor. Soon his reports started getting vague.

I also observed other behaviors. I noticed that he constantly asked me the same questions. One thing in particular was how to set the washing machine to wash and to adjust the water level.

"Where's the water knob?" He'd ask.

"It's the little, silver knob on the left. Turn it to the right. Stop after one click on medium."

"Which knob do I use to wash?"

"The large silver one," I said. I pointed to the knob.

"Do I turn it or push it?"

I replied, "First, push the knob in. Turn it to the right. Stop on fourteen. Then pull it."

I turned and saw a very satisfied look on his face as he heard the water pouring into the tub. I smiled and nodded my head. He tickled me under the arm playfully and made me laugh. A few days later, I decided to write the instructions and tape them on the machine. This worked for a few weeks.

Peter started to get frustrated when he was unable to find things that he misplaced in the house. I tried to comfort him. "We're both getting older," I'd say. We have to take our time and just relax. Give ourselves more time to figure things out."

We maintained our normal routine for a couple of years, but the memory problems worsened. I took my husband to my general practitioner. The doctor examined him. Dr. Wayland felt Peter was experiencing adjustment problems.

The doctor said, "Mr. Daniels, you have recently made some dramatic changes in life. You got married. You retired from your job. You relocated. That's a lot."

My husband said, "I was ready. I'm happy here."

Dr. Wayland prescribed a medication that helped him relax. The doctor said he needed to calm himself and focus on his new beginnings. Stay cool and remember age sixty-two brought on natural changes. We have to take it easy. The doctor said it was a lot easier to get agitated over little things when one gets older.

Peter's demeanor improved. He appeared more at peace. For a while, he bounced back to the jovial, sweet, loving man that I married. I loved him so much. I was glad to see the change. I restructured our day to include activities that fostered short-term memory and boosted self-esteem. I did this because I had read about techniques and methods that enhanced memory. One of the most important things suggested was to do things that built on strengths. I also kept in mind things he enjoyed doing.

We bowled almost daily. He was a three hundred point bowler. We both bowled on leagues in the past. I established my game again, but I was comfortable and happy when he won. The excitement of kicking up that left leg and swinging his right arm made my day. He was a true competitor. When his children came to visit, bowling was definitely on the agenda. He was the king of bowling and it was evidenced in his behavior. He scored higher than everybody.

Something else was a few weekly trips to the golf course. He loved playing golf. He was an excellent putter. He made the most outstanding putts I'd ever seen. Every now and then, he went on the driving range. He didn't enjoy driving the ball as much as putting, however, he'd hit the ball over two hundred and fifty feet easily.

I took him to the Center for Aging in Goldsboro. He liked it when the teacher did math. He'd answer a question or two, but he was not interested in the worksheets. He participated in the games because he loves socializing. He did not play checkers, but I remember when he'd beat me at every game. I was pretty good. I never did figure out how to win a game. He had no pity even when we played four or five consecutive games. My major concern was to fill every day with activities or events for his entertainment and well being.

At this point, I reflected on comments his children made shortly after we got married. They asked if I noticed that he was forgetful. They said that he didn't used to be that way. He'd promised something and forgot to do it. He'd put something down and forgot where it was. I told them I was having trouble remembering. Memory changes when one gets older. You walk in a room for something. You just stand there because it takes a minute to remember why you're there. Don't put keys down. You won't remember where you put them until moments later. Also, reading becomes a problem. One has to extend the book away from the face at arm's length to see. Otherwise, the words look like one big blur. There was nothing remarkable about his memory.

Several months later, the effectiveness of the medication for relaxation declined. I recognized mood swings. One minute he was amiable and caring. The next minute he was jittery and angry.

Chapter Nine

Is This Yours or Mine?

The joy of the Lord was our strength (Nehemiah 8:10), and we looked to God, who was a very present help in the time of trouble (Psalm 46:1). We loved talking about Jesus and all of the wonderful things that He continued to do in our lives. Sometimes, when we were at the table eating, my Baby would reach for my bowl of cereal. I ate it in a burgundy bowl and had a white, plastic cup from which I drank. I liked that little cup, because it was the one I'd gotten when I stumped the clown who tried to guess my age at Carowinds.

My chair didn't face the TV like Peter's did, but I liked it that way. I swallowed the three pills for the morning and took my pill box back to the bedroom. When I came back, my Baby was sitting in my chair, eating my cereal.

"Why are you in my chair?" His blue bowl, filled with cereal, and his red plastic cup were at his place.

Peter shrugged and spooned in another bite. "Why don't you sit down?"

I tossed my hands in the air.

"You're eating my cereal. That one has my soy milk in it. Remember?"

"It does?" He looked at the bowl.

"Is that yours or mine?"

"I don't know."

I recalled having finished eating breakfast one morning and leaving my pills on the table. I forgot to take them, because the phone rang and I answered it. When I returned to take the medicine, the pills were gone. My Baby had taken my pills. I had Norvasc, Lipitor, and Oscal 500+D. I watched him closely to see if he started sweating or getting weak. I knew if I noticed those signs, I needed to rush him to the emergency room.

What was going on? I needed to be extremely watchful and careful around him. I began thinking about his memory problems. Thank God none of the pills were harmful—it could've killed him. I came to understand that our life was beginning to be quite different. It appeared that one minute, things would be normal and the next minute change into an oh-my-goodness state.

I took all of those things in stride. I kept saying, "My Baby is just my baby, that's all." There was a memorable, sunny morning and we were dressing to go walking in the neighborhood. I had everything on but my sneakers. I searched everywhere but was unable to find them. Peter was dressed and ready to walk out of the door. He was merely standing there waiting for me. I just happened to look him over, and when I did, there were my shoes. My Baby had on my sneakers. It was funny because I didn't even know that he could wear them. His were too big for me, so I had to ask him to let me wear those that he had on.

I hurried to the bedroom to get his sneakers.

"Here Baby. Put these on. They match your sweat suit."

He stood there. He glanced at the shoes and back at his clothes.

"That really goes together. Wow. What do you think?" No reply.

He sat down with a confused look. I bent down and took the shoes off. I put his shoes on. I put my shoes on. We left without a word. On the way to the track, I asked, "You okay?" He said, "Yea."

I could see that Peter couldn't discern the difference. He actually thought he had on his own sneakers. I started reading more and more about dementia and learned that memory loss was due to brain cells dying. It caused people to be unable to recognize things, read words, or find their way back home if they were alone. His symptoms matched a specific type of dementia—Alzheimer's disease. I observed more carefully and read more frequently.

Some of the typical symptoms include: mismanaging finances; losing writing and drawing skills; losing perceptual skills and visual acuity; declining temporal concepts (telling time, knowing time and dates); following instructions, and driving unsafely. Imaginations run rampant replacing reality with fantasy.

We went to Dr. Jessup, Peter's ophthalmologist, for his six-month checkup. The receptionist gave us a form to sign. I took the pen and started to sign.

She said, "He has to sign. He's the patient."

I reminded her of the appointment letter on file from the clerk of superior court designating me as his general guardian.

"He has to sign. All he has to do is write his name."

I got irritated. "Miss, evidently you failed to hear what I said. I repeat, I am his general guardian. For your information, this lets most people in your position know that I have legal authority to sign his name."

She stood there with the form and pen in her hand. She had the gall to say, "He has to sign. You cannot sign his name."

I was furious, but cool. The waiting room was full.

"Put the form on the counter," I demanded.

"Sign the form Baby."

She saw his signature. She was so unpolished, unprofessional, and uneducated. She actually said, "Sir, you did not finish." I took my husband by the hand and told her, "That's it. Take it or leave it."

I was livid. She embarrassed him because his face was red. I wanted to climb across that counter, grab her in the collar, and slap her face from side to side until I was unable to lift my hand anymore. That feeling rose up in me by surprise. The whole time I was in school from elementary through college, I never fought. I used my mouth to defend myself. The thought of getting physical was beneath by character.

I wondered what this meant. Was this the ebb tide or a brewing storm?

Chapter Ten

My Poor Troubled Baby

I wondered what was going on in my Baby's mind when he went to the garage and just stood there. I got the impression that he was searching for something. He just looked at me when he realized that I'd opened the door, curious about his whereabouts. I sometimes would ask him, "Baby, what are you doing?"

"Nothing."

He liked to sit in his green Cadillac and piddle around. He spent hours opening and closing the trunk, as if he were looking for something. I'd inquire about what was going on. Sometimes he'd tell me that he was looking for his golf balls, golf shoes, or cap. He really loved caps and usually carried around three or four. Regardless of where we were going, my Baby would have a cap on his head and two or three in his hands. At times, he would actually change caps while we were away from home visiting family. He always carried his travel kit, too. He had it packed with important stuff. He loved to put his address book, belts, newspaper articles, pictures, and then the usual toiletry items in his kit.

At times, I wished that I could just make sense of what was going on with him. I remembered reading that dementia affected the brain cells controlling one's spatial and reasoning abilities. That could possibly be the reason for the length of time he spent in front of the mirror when he combed his hair. He loved to look good, and he'd spend long hours in front of the mirror. Even though it was common habit, it had gotten worse.

I mused over this. There were times when I would ask him to open the lift gate of the van, and he'd complain about how lifting hurt his shoulders. If lifting hurt his shoulders, how could he stand in front of the mirror combing his hair without pain? I don't think he made the connection. Or maybe he just didn't want to be bothered.

My Baby loved attention, too. When we went shopping, he would start rubbing his shoulder with his hand. One day in Lowe's, he was rubbing his shoulder so much it caught the eyes of the cashier as we were checking out. I handed her the money, but she didn't take it. My Baby captivated her.

The cashier stated, "I know what he's going through. I have arthritis, too." She finally took the money.

When we got to the car, I asked him if he were really, really in pain. His face looked flushed, and he told me he was.

I asked, "Is it the left or right shoulder?"

"Both."

"How bad is the pain?"

He shook his head and responded, "Bad. I'm hurting bad."

76

I made an appointment at the VAH. After all, his mom had arthritis. His doctor ordered X-rays, and the results were negative regarding inflammation, which would've been present in his joints if he'd had the condition. His primary care physician added pain medication to Peter's prescriptions.

We were still carrying on with as much normalcy as possible, but now and again, I detected how much of a "little child" he would revert to in the presence of his mom. One day we took a ride to enjoy the scenery. He started speaking so softly, I could hardly hear him. I told him to clear his throat so that I could hear and understand what he was saying. He really sounded like he had a frog in his throat—a gravely bullfrog.

I became aware of that voice when we'd visit his mom. She babied him so much. When she complained about arthritis, he'd say he hurts. Sometimes I got so tickled that I'd just sit there. Her reaction was usually the same. She'd pour on the motherly attention. I didn't understand how she heard him due to the childish talking and gesturing. Finally, I arrived at the conclusion that he fathomed illness and timidity in order to get positive attention from his mom.

Maybe it was a cunning way to distract. When she started talking, it was almost impossible to interrupt her to make a comment. A conversation about her arthritis and pains would turn into how she didn't sleep much, and how her legs hurt, and how the trees got this white stuff growing on them, and how this stuff is diseased and killing her trees and shrubbery.

She would rattle on that this white stuff wasn't just in her yard, but it was also in the neighbors' yard, other yards in other cities, other yards in other states, and maybe all over the world. She would tell us that nothing happened just to be happening. There had to be a reason for everything and all this stuff dying like it was. There was something going on, and we didn't understand it. It wasn't meant for us to understand it.

In fact, it wasn't meant for us to understand anything 'cause people got sick, and we didn't know why. Doctors didn't even know why, and people died. We were all gonna die of something. We didn't know what, and we just had to go on 'cause whatever happened was going to happen. We couldn't do anything to stop it or change it.

Mrs. Daniels was a cute little, short lady. She'd be in her lounge chair talking up something. Peter sat on the sofa with his eyes closed. I'd listen without saying a word. I nodded occasionally. Every now and then, she'd go to the kitchen and look out the window, but she kept on talking. She didn't miss a beat. We just can't. We couldn't be worried about this and that, first one thing then another. And it didn't matter how good or bad you were, things just happened.

Why, I knew some folk who didn't hurt anybody, never harmed a hair on anybody's head, but they got killed. They just died, and they couldn't help it. Neither could we. Things just happened! I tried to treat everybody nice and did the best I could to do right by folks. A cop told me one time that if everybody was as nice and good as I was, there wouldn't be any need for policemen. My mother-in-law was something else; she could really talk, and she thought she was quiet.

It was difficult to change the subject. If you stood up as if to leave, she would stand with you and keep on talking. I found out if anyone wanted to talk about church, they would be talking by themselves.

There was one summer that my Baby and I traveled over three thousand miles crossing eleven states while on vacation. Peter was still driving then, but not very much. I drove all of those miles with the exception of the last few miles between Virginia and Goldsboro. We thoroughly enjoyed our vacation, and we took many, many pictures.

My mother-in-law wanted to hear about that trip. We enjoyed the sights and family events along the way. We stopped in New Jersey for the christening of little Melonie, Nathan and Samantha's daughter. We saw all of the children and grandchildren while we were there. Church service was very good; and the family dinner afterward was especially nice.

We met one of my longtime girlfriends in Branson, Missouri. We tried to visit one another once every ten years or so. There were some questionable behaviors that my girlfriend mentioned to me during the time spent in Branson. She was a social work supervisor. She mentioned how Peter sat on the car seat while it was in a folded position. He didn't bother to unfold the seat before sitting down on it. I noticed it, but he said he was fine, so I let it be.

Another reason for the trip was to help celebrate the start of my brother's new church in Illinois. He was the founding pastor of the church and my whole family was there for the grand occasion. All my mother-in-law asked about the trip was how we did not get sick of all that driving. She wanted to know if it was annoying to stay in so many motels and to have to be around so many strange people all that time.

While we were in church, Peter kept staring at folk, and it became quite obvious when the women started approaching him after church. It was as if he had gone to church in Illinois by himself. That was very embarrassing for me. Somehow, someway, he wandered back. This behavior started a pattern of similar actions in other churches and in other public places.

His reasoning ability declined. The part of the brain that controlled impulses was beginning to show sharp declination. I remember reading that these impulses were centered in the frontal lobe of the brain. All I knew was that it was time for me to seek more medical advice.

Chapter Eleven

Seeking a Medical Diagnosis

Aging was a subject that I thought about often. It affected us all. The more I read about the aging process, the better my understanding became regarding both of us. Some reports stated that there was a decline in the ability to taste. That made me chuckle, because now I realized why lots of us in our sixties gain weight. Other reports stated that there was a decline in weight due to a loss of lean tissue, water, and bone.

One third of men and half of all women over age sixty-five reported having some form of arthritis. Even though we hadn't been diagnosed with this, we couldn't seem to tolerate much cold weather. My reaction time had slowed down. I heard what one was saying, but I just didn't feel like moving right then. I had to urinate more often, and Peter did, as well. This was a problem, because I never wanted to leave the sanctuary in case I missed something important. I hated to receive secondhand information.

I noticed some older folk making a beeline for the bathroom, and I found out why. Some of us developed incontinence, dribbling, and frequency of urination. If one didn't want to get knocked down, he needed to get out of the path to the restroom. The rapid pounding of walking canes was a force to be reckoned with.

I talked to my Baby when we returned from our trip and mentioned the behaviors that were unlike any I had observed before. It upset him.

I asked, "Where did you go when you left the visitor's center at my brother's church?"

"Nowhere."

"You went out of the room, Peter," I said.

"I didn't."

I told him he left again when they had the repasts. He denied having done the things that I was talking about and became quite angry. I stopped the conversation. I began to talk about more pleasant subjects, and he calmed right down.

"I enjoyed the trip, didn't you?"

"Yes."

"I'm thankful to God for blessing my baby brother in such a marvelous way."

"It was a big church," he said.

"I appreciated the teenage steppers. What an innovative way to involve the youth in church."

Here again was the presence of mood swings and anger, so I could see the pattern of established behavior. Peter was unable to remember or was in denial. This was serious. I needed professional advice. What if he walked away with someone's spouse? What would happen if he were unable to find his way back? What if some mean person would perceive that behavior as aggression and feel empowered to hurt him? I had lots of questions. I began to feel that I was losing this gentle, kind-hearted, soft spoken man to an unforeseen illness.

I went to the civilian doctor who prescribed Lexapro for Peter. Upon describing the behaviors to the doctor, he felt a psychiatric examination was the next step. He made the appointment, and we went. The psychiatrist interviewed Peter as I observed in the examination room. I was anxious, but very attentive. I needed some answers.

When my husband spoke, it was hard to catch his words. That was the first time I noticed it. The doctor recommended a neurological exam, and I told her Peter was a veteran receiving medical treatments at the VAH. I made an appointment with his geriatrician.

About this time, my husband started telling me that he wanted me to handle the business; he was no longer interested and didn't really feel like dealing with people on that level. I told him that I would need to get a power of attorney. I went to an attorney who specialized in senior affairs and he told me that he needed to talk to both of us together. When I mentioned that my husband was in treatment for memory difficulties, he told me that he needed a statement from his doctor in order to proceed with legal papers.

In the meantime, I decided to write his children to let them know what was going on with their dad. We talked by phone a few days later. They were very concerned and asked me to keep them informed.

We kept the appointment at the VAH with the geriatrician. The doctor was very kind, and so was the nurse practitioner.

They greeted him with a smile and a handshake.

"Have a seat, Mr. Daniels. You look nice today. How are you feeling?"

Peter nodded his head.

"Are you in any pain?"

"No."

"You having trouble remembering?"

"Yes."

"We lose our ability to recall events and activities as easily as we used to as we grow older. This is common for all of us. Sometimes we do better than at other times. We want to help you with your memory. To do that, we start with a series of questions. Do you mind?"

"No."

Ms. Johnson, the nurse practitioner, asked the questions. She was careful not to rush. She gave him time to respond. She would ask if he had finished before going to the next question. Halfway through, he relaxed. She complimented him as he progressed through the test. He gave verbal responses and did a few drawings. Memory loss was evidenced by the results. The doctor prescribed Aricept. We were told to return in three months to take the Mini Mental State Exam (MMSE) again.

I held my husband in my arms and just sat with him. We talked about old times—when we'd first met. He seemed to cheer up when we'd talked about things back then. When he wanted to do so, I would encourage him to talk about his children and grandchildren.

Three months later, in November of 2005, we returned, and Peter was given the MMSE again. The score was six points below his original score. The doctor was stunned at the rapidity of his inability to respond to the same test items as before.

The doctor said to me, "The drawings were good the first time. They were not discernable this time."

I looked at them.

He said, "Responses to 'list items' were very low."

The doctor reported not having experienced such a re-markable difference and referred Peter to the neuropsy-chologist at the VAH. I asked the doctor to change Peter's medication, since his memory continued to decline. The new medication was Namenda.

Driving license renewal was approaching in February 2006, and I started preparing him in December. I got the driver's book and made the signs out of tag board like I'd used in schools to make bulletin boards. I drew the pictures on one side and printed the words on the opposite side. We studied using the flash card method. We would practice for ten-minute intervals twice a day, two to three times a week.

When the testing time came, we prayed and went to the highway patrol office for the test. I interceded on behalf of my husband asking the examiner to be patient with him, allowing him extra time. She assured me that he could have all of the time he needed. They didn't rush anyone, especially their senior citizens. We stayed about an hour. At first, he appeared to be doing fine. He looked into the machine and answered the questions. He stopped responding. He looked and smiled but didn't talk. I got nervous. The examiner called for me, and she pulled me aside to ask me what was wrong. I simply told her that he was easily distracted. I smiled at him and returned to the waiting area.

"Mr. Daniels," she said, "Take this sheet and study the signs a bit longer."

He nodded his head, took the sheet, and moved to the study area.

The examiner said, "I will call you back."

After about thirty minutes, she called him back. She sent for me and told me that she felt he didn't comprehend.

As we were leaving, another examiner was so touched, she called to me,

"Mam, I will test him. Maybe he will do better with someone else. I've seen it happen."

"Thank you," I responded, "But I feel he'd been through enough this morning and was exhausted."

I told her I'd bring him back on another day. I thanked her and left. I was as hurt as he was. Probably even more so.

At this point, I felt as if he wasn't fully attuned to the gravity of the situation. I certainly was. On the way home,

I stopped and treated him to one of his favorite meals—a burger and fries from McDonald's. Later that day, we went bowling. This lifted his spirit. It certainly did mine.

A few days later, I asked him if he were ready to start studying again for his license. His response shed new-found insight concerning his condition. He felt as if he'd done his best the first time around and he didn't want to go through it again.

"I tried. I really did."

"You don't want to try again?"

He shook his head. . .no.

I hurt for him, but there was no way that I could possibly feel the pain that I saw in his eyes. I hugged him, gave him a big kiss, and took him to the golf course to do some putting. Even this was recognition of something lost. Remembering the game was too challenging, and the most he could do was putt or go on the driving range. He still enjoyed doing that, and I was delighted.

The most disheartening facet about golfing was how his buddies were so uneasy around him, that the patience to assist him in playing just wasn't a part of their personas. Going through that with my Baby made me see how fearful and uneasy some folk were around people with dementia. I felt they didn't know what to do or say. Withdrawal was the only technique they knew.

I prayed every night and throughout the day. I wanted God to carry me through this with the compassion and empathy I needed to care for my husband. I desired to be that pillar he yearned for during this crucial time of his life. I asked God for wisdom. I had to keep my joy—unspeakable joy. I remembered Psalm 46:1: *God is our refuge and strength, a very present help in trouble.*

In April, it was time for the appointment with the neuropsychologist. The doctor was cordial and gentle. He walked into the waiting room with a very friendly smile. He spoke and shook hands. He talked with my husband on the way to his office. The tense feeling left Peter by the time we got to the office.

Dr. Barnwell was very thorough in his questions and explanations. He made my husband feel so at ease, I was able to relax, as well. I did what I normally did, asked a myriad of questions. He answered them all. Mostly, I was concerned about the overall effect of this disease on our lifestyle. We covered questions about finances, medical care, spousal interactions, emotional changes, behavioral changes, in-home care, and resources to obtain additional information and assistance.

The doctor scheduled the neuropsychological test later that month. The compelling results confirmed the presence of profound memory loss, as well as significant brain damage. Dr. Barnwell recommended that we go to court to obtain a general guardianship appointment by a superior court judge. This would give me the legal rights to handle all business and medical matters pertaining to my Baby. He suggested we see a neurologist at Duke.

His geriatrician made the appointment. This doctor was transferred to another hospital; consequently, the follow-up treatment at the VAH was done in another clinic with another geriatrician. I had no problems with the change since I understand how the military makes assignments. Peter appeared to be fine. I was aware of the "white coat syndrome" experienced when patients go to see their doctor. I felt that feeling was okay. I perceived no evidence to the contrary. This new physician, Dr. Zeculaw, followed my husband through all of the remaining treatment procedures.

In August 2006, we went to court and the superior court judge granted the petition for general guardianship. I was appointed as Peter's legal guardian and was made responsible for making an annual report to the court regarding business dealings for the year.

We did go to Duke Hospital, and my husband was treated by a neurologist. He conducted some tests that showed that my Baby was in the ninety-five percent of the general population, where there was no absolute cause known for the onset of dementia or Alzheimer's disease.

The fact was that we were seeing the best doctors in the northeastern part of Carolina. The VAH and Duke had impeccable reputations, and Peter continued to be a recipient of their expertise. I was so thankful and grateful that we resided in such a rich medical community.

References

Mayo Clinic. Aging: What to Expect. http://www.mayoclinic.org/healthy-living/healthy-aging/in-depth/aging/art-20046070 - 41k

Wikipedia contributors, "Aging," Wikipedia, The Free Encyclopedia, http://en.wikipedia.org/w/index.php?title=Aging&oldid=527945955 (accessed June 12, 2014).

Chapter Twelve

A Spiritual Awakening

What a joy it was to be in the service of the Lord. We attended St. Matthews United Holy Church. The church was founded more than a year ago by a dear cohort in the Lord. After a dynamic message, the altar appeal was made, and several people went for prayer. I was so elated when I saw my husband at the altar. I began to pray that the Lord would grant whatever petition he prayed for on that day. My heart was so heavy for him with all that he was going through.

I was especially moved to see him at the altar because it was a Eucharistic Day celebrating the Lord Jesus, and I wanted my husband's heart to be right with God. While the preacher was praying for my husband—Peter raised his hands and praised the Lord. It wasn't a matter of just moving his lips silently, I could hear him praising God as if he really didn't care who heard him.

Oh, how this just filled my spirit with joy. I moved to Peter and touched him. I joined with him in supplication to God. I knew when one prayed out of a sincere heart that God heard and answered prayer.

This was a critical time of worship. People needed to be sincere. The results were very serious; and the Bible was clear on the subject. One could drink damnation to his own soul by coming forth and partaking in the wrong spirit. The actual test came when one declared in his testimony that he'd accepted the Lord as his personal Savior and he no longer indulged in the same lifestyle. I knew this could make the devil mad and that he'd attack the individual. The imps jumped on my husband, and by the time he got home that day, he could hardly move his arms. His heart was palpitating.

I explained to him that this was a trick of the devil. Peter needed to denounce satan with his own mouth; speak to that devil.

"Get thee behind me in the name of Jesus. Satan, you have no dominion here. I plead the blood of Jesus."

"In the name of Jesus."

"In the name of Jesus."

"I plead the blood."

My husband spoke those words, and within about twenty minutes, the pain left him. His heart rhythm returned to normal. The Word of God says in Psalm 46:5, *"God is in the midst of her; she shall not be moved: God shall help her and that right early."*

God manifested Himself to my husband amazingly that afternoon, and I was glad. I was spiritually excited, because God had responded to my husband. This let him know that God was real. God could do all things and would do whatever one asks Him to do if he prayed not amiss.

I reminisced about all that my Baby was going through mentally and emotionally, as he lived through the most debilitating time of this disease—losing his dignity and independence by not being able to drive. Before he lost his license, there were several incidents that caused alarm and fear on the road when he drove. I recalled one night he was driving from Charlie C's grocery store and got to the traffic light that was green. He just stopped under the light.

Peter looked from right to left.

"I don't know what to do," he said.

"Press the accelerator Baby. Keep going in the same direction."

He was so uneasy. Fortunately, no cars were coming. Reluctantly, he proceeded to move forward, looking scared and nervous. I was tense too.

At other times when he drove, he would suddenly stop the car on the road and look confused. Sometimes he would get angry, because people would start blowing their horns. He wouldn't let me drive in most instances. He just wanted me to tell him what to do. I would tell him, being careful to keep calm and to speak slowly and gently.

I started getting concerned about what would happen if I were not with him. So, I finally convinced him not to drive unless I was with him. He agreed, but he'd say,

"I am not crazy. I can still drive."

I would smile. "I know Baby."

One day we were riding and came to a six-lane highway near the mall. He just asked me if I wanted to drive. I told him where to pull over, and I took the wheel. Right at that moment, I felt my husband had reached the conclusion that his driving ability was so seriously impaired that he was putting our lives in danger by continuing to drive. Some folk with physical disabilities can keep driving due to the fact that their cars can be redesigned to accommodate that handicap. My husband, on the other hand, had no recourse.

The Lord would always put the most appropriate words in my mouth to soothe him in difficult moments. I told him that he was a privileged person, because he had a chauffeur who would take him anywhere he wanted to go free of charge. He could just sit in the car and order me to do whatever he wanted me to do. That cheered him up, because I'd tell him how hard other men had it and how easy he had it. Just sitting in the car taking in all of the scenery. I finally convinced him to return to the driver's license agency to get an identification card. I told him the card could be used the same way he used the Veterans Identification Card. The day that we got that card, his spirits lifted. I was glad he got it.

We are settling down now and hoping to enjoy a life together with the recognition that things would never be quite the same anymore. But we loved each other and were determined to keep loving Jesus and pressing our way.

Chapter Thirteen

Hunker Down

We hunkered down for the night because of inclement weather. I still practiced the same traditions I was taught as a little girl—get quiet and be still. Peter and I had had a wonderful day, and I was tired. The television had long been cut off, and there was a sense of calm. My Baby roamed through the house. I wondered why, but I just stayed put and observed.

After a few minutes, Peter rattled some keys. I arose to see what was going on, and he had the car keys in his hands. I just looked and didn't say anything. Shortly thereafter, he told me he was going to drive to his mom's house. She only lived a couple of blocks away, but since it was 2:00 a.m., I suggested that we wait until later that morning. He wasn't taking no for an answer.

At least I didn't have to get dressed. Sometimes when I had a problem getting Peter dressed for bed, I would just keep my clothes on as well.

"Baby, let's wait until daybreak. The rain has stopped, but it's pitch dark."

"Mama isn't sleep."

"We might frighten her knocking on her door this time of day. Let's lie down and rest."

"I'm going. You don't have to take me."

He let me know that if I didn't want to take him that he'd walk over there. That time of day, I didn't think he was serious. I was wrong. After I convinced him to give me the keys, he opened the door and started walking down the street in the direction of his mom's.

I ran behind him trying to change his mind about walking, telling him to return that I would drive. He just kept right on walking. He totally ignored me. Instead of walking with him, I ran back to the house, got the car, and pulled up beside him. He would not get in no matter how much I tried to convince him. I drove slowly beside him to ensure that he arrived safely.

When we arrived at his mom's, he knocked on the door. She asked who it was, and he told her Peter. She wondered what was going on, and I told her that he was having trouble getting to bed and wanted to come to her house. She was already aware of various behaviors that I had mentioned to her.

Mrs. Daniels turned to her son and said, "I love you Peter. You know you can come to my house anytime. I'd rather you come during the day, but not by yourself. I want you to do what Toni tells you. It's for your own good."

"Do you hear me, son?"

Peter nodded his head. I was distraught and worried. I hoped he'd understood.

"Toni was simply trying to protect you and make sure that you were safe."

"Mrs. Daniels, it has become quite difficult; I have to keep him in my presence at all times."

She said to Peter, "I know Toni is trying to keep you at home just as long as she possibly can. She doesn't want to put you in a nursing home."

As he sat in her lounge chair, she said to him, "If you keep wandering off that way, then Toni will not have any choice."

She inquired as to whether or not he had been wandering away from home in Fayetteville, and I admitted that he had, but that he'd found his way back home. It scared me to death, but I didn't act like it. I just said to him, "I see that you went for a little walk, huh."

I watched him more closely when he was in the yard after that incident. Some of our neighbors were outside, and they were watching him. He walked about a block up the street and came back. I actually watched him as he was returning home.

There were a couple of other incidents regarding driving. One Saturday afternoon, I was cooking at our home in Goldsboro, and my Baby decided he wanted to go to his mom's. When we were in Goldsboro, we would go to her house just about every day. We hadn't made it over that day, yet. I wanted to eat first so that we could take our medications. He was not ready to hear that. He started getting angry.

I just stopped cooking and took him. I returned home and finished preparing the meal. Later, I picked him up, and we ate supper.

It wasn't hard for me to relate to him about the inability to drive. After driving on the autobahn in Germany for three years, it was very difficult for me to remember I was back in the States—I was still driving seventy to eighty miles an hour on the highway. I had my driver's license revoked for speeding more than fifteen miles over the speed limit. It wasn't fun having to depend on someone else to take you places. This happened in 1982.

Things with Peter continued to get worse. I learned to hide the car keys, but one day Peter wanted them. When he couldn't find the keys, he got so angry that he started going in and out of the house talking loudly and slamming the front door. It frightened me when I was unable to calm him down.

He kept getting louder and louder. When I saw that look of terror on his face, I called the police. When they arrived, I explained what had happened. I also told them that he had dementia. Peter had settled down and was sitting in a chair in the middle bedroom. He wasn't talking, but he was still mad.

I'll never forget that immense feeling of compassion. I was so choked up I could hardly talk. The more I tried to explain the situation, the more choked up I became. I was so hurt, because I was sensing his deep feeling of inadequacy. Peter was a grown man but unable to perform basic tasks. How demeaning that must have felt.

The male cop gave him advice about his behavior. He told him that acting out that way would land him in jail. Those words really irritated Peter. I could see the anger on his face. I cried over the situation. My voice was so low that it was hardly above a whisper. I was trying to help, but it felt as if I hurt him more.

The police woman was not as curt. Her compassion eased the edginess.

She said to him, "Your wife loves you. She was trying to help you to be safe."

"Sir, do you understand what I'm saying?"

"Yes," Peter replied.

"Were you planning to harm your wife?"

"No."

"Will you promise not to try to drive your car?"

"Yes."

She asked, "Will you stay home with your wife?"

"Yes."

The male cop asked me, "Do you want us to take him with us?"

"No, because he has calmed down and I felt like I would be okay."

I thanked them. They told me to call back if things changed.

That was the first time his behavior had frightened me in our home. There was another time when he was driving. The engine revved as he accelerated. He continued to increase the speed. I asked him what was going on, and he told me he was trying to catch up to the car ahead of us. That confused me, because we had no idea who the people were. He finally slowed down.

When I drove fast, I was usually alone, but being in the car with someone else driving fast was quite uncomfortable. I was glad paying the heavy fine and being without a license had taught me a lesson a few years ago.

Calling the police taught my husband a valuable lesson, too. I never had the occasion to call them again; thank the Lord. He did let me know that he didn't like it. He kept bringing it up over and over and over again. He talked about it for a very long time. I was just thankful that I could use that "ace in the hole" anytime I needed to do so.

Chapter Fourteen

Spousal Symbiosis

Husbands and wives become so bound to one another that some people say they start to look and act alike. I can say that we started to talk alike and could read each other's minds. We could even finish the other person's sentence and be right on the mark. It was strange, but most folk have experienced some form of what I called a transformation of interpersonal relationships.

When I recalled my science classes, symbiotic relationships came to mind. It always intrigued me to study about animals even though I really did not like science that much. It just amazed me how much alike homosapiens were to the lower classes of animals. I enjoyed watching shows about animals on Animal Kingdom.

Symbiosis, as I remembered, was a close relationship that occurred when two or more animals or plants of dissimilar species lived together. In this relationship one or more of the members benefitted from the others. In some instances, animals and plants were observed as they interacted with inanimate objects.

There were several types studied; however, four lingered with me. Mutualism was where two or more organisms benefitted from each other. A good example was the bee that collected pollen from the seed plant and spread the pollen to another plant. Thus, the pollination fertilized the plant. Both benefitted. The bee did what the plant could not do. The plant needed the bee for the completion of the pollination stage.

The second type was Neutralism where neither species benefitted or was harmed. Both organisms were unaffected. Two kinds of fishes were good examples—the flounder and the catfish. They coexisted in the water, but they fed on different kinds of organisms.

Commensalism was the third one studied. This relationship was somewhat different because it involved animate and inanimate objects and only one benefitted. The other was unaffected. This seemed unfair to me but when I mused over the specifications and possibilities, one prime example came to mind. Ever since I could remember there was a bird nest on top of one of the wooden posts that were used to support the front porch of our house. I watched the birds fly back and forth as they sang and chirped. The little baby birds squeaked, peeked, and moved busily about in their nest as they eagerly awaited their mother to bring them food.

Well, what made the birds, their nest, and the house so commensally related was that the birds gendered all of the benefits. The house got absolutely nothing out of it. The birds were protected from the weather.

Peter and I fell into this category. Even though my Baby and I were the same species, he'd been infested by unknown organisms in our environment that caused him to be unable to produce in ways that benefited me as the other member of this spousal symbiosis. This resulted in having to resort to behaviors that were dysfunctional. This was precisely pertinent regarding intimacy and romanticism. While an individual may experience gross imaginations watching television, it did not include the partner. It may have fulfilled one's conjugal needs, but the other individual was omitted. Perhaps the brain functioning did not allow for the cognitive recognition of the need that existed. Other interdependent pleasures went lacking as well.

Mutualism was undoubtedly the most rewarding symbiosis where both benefitted equally. We reaped those benefits early in our marriage. Then came the drenching, the soaking that pulled us away emotionally from our cozy little world of familiarity.

The most profound experience happened relationally with the Lord. A deeper, closer bond was established. I drank of His blood and ate of His body in remembrance of His work for both of us on the Cross of Calvary. First Corinthians 11:26 says, *"For as often as ye eat this bread and drink this cup, ye do show the Lord's death 'til He comes."* I stayed in His presence communing with Him day and night.

Now, the fourth and final symbiotic relationship was Parasitism. It depicted one species benefitting while the other one was harmed. This relationship had no affect on us. A good example of it was like a tick sucking the blood of the animal and causing an infectious wound.

I thank God that I never felt that our relationship became parasitistic. Things had changed, but we were still in love, drinking the blood of the Lamb. For it was that blood that gave me life. It was that blood that washed and cleansed. It was that blood that gave hope. It was that blood that gave joy unspeakable and full of glory. It was that blood. It was that blood. It was that blood. It was that blood.

References

"Symbiotic Relations," Encyclopaedia Britannica, Inc., Volume 11: Solovyov-Truck, 15th Edition, January 1990.

Wikipedia contributors, "Symbiosis," Wikipedia, The Free Encyclopedia, http://en.wikipedia.org/w/index.php?title=Symbiosis&oldid=612352455 (accessed May 2010).

III.

Reflecting
and Projecting

Chapter Fifteen

Why This Marriage?

For fifteen years, I lived single, loving Jesus, and going on with my profession as a school counselor in the Bladen County School System. I thoroughly enjoyed my job. I was a member of St. Thomas Church and was president of the Holy Young People's Union.

I had many opportunities to be married, one in particular where a pastor in the Baptist movement came to my school to ask me to marry him. He told me he had money and lots of it. He told me how he was an administrator of the General Baptist Convention and how he traveled all over the world. He wanted someone to accompany him on those trips, and I would be the perfect match for him. "Not only are you pretty to look at," he told me, "You have a beautiful spirit." The other Sunday when you came to my church to invite us to fellowship with your church, you stayed right on the subject. No matter how hard I attempted to get you off key, you stayed focused. You just kept talking about doing the Lord's work and how you were on a mission purposed, planned, and directed by God. You let me know that you were not your own, you were sold out for Jesus. All in all that drew me to you even more."

I'd only seen the pastor one time at that brief visit on that particular Sunday.

"I'm not here to redirect your course; I just want to add happiness, money, travel, and clothes."

He told me he would fly me to foreign countries just to have lunch with him and would see to it that I got back home by nightfall on the same day. He just wanted to have me with him. He would not try to keep me away from my Kingdom building agenda. He told me that I could have not only money, but my own bank account and as many credit cards as I wanted. All he wanted was me.

There were others, but I always managed to put Christ in front of me and any desire for natural things. After all, I was in my forties and as strong-willed as ever. I felt this way because I reshaped most of my childhood virtues and was now comfortable with the person that I'd become. I'd gone through the process of shaking and breaking those barriers that might have held me back. The Lord had remolded and refurbished me. I was no longer momma or daddy's little girl. And I certainly didn't have to try to prove anything to anybody. I was who I was. Take it or leave it.

It was nice to have offers, but none of them were quite right. My whole countenance changed when I heard Peter say, "This is Peter." Prior to that, I was very strong and willing to tell folk no, because I didn't want them taking up my personal time and space. I had things to do. But, that time, I was open and eager to mingle with Peter.

After I learned that I could get married and not burn in hell because my ex-spouse was still living, I had a choice to make. Did I want to marry Peter or should I wait for another? Was it time to stop playing and get serious? I knew right away that he was the one. It had never become so clear to me in the Scripture that I could remarry, and I just had this real sense of peace.

Now, after a couple of years into the marriage, I began to realize that this was not a normal marriage. There was something wrong. I discovered some psychological issues, but due to my counseling background, I felt this had something to do with the reason we ended up together. I really felt the Lord had made it so crystal clear in my mind and had given me so much peace because I was the right partner for Peter. I wouldn't judge my Baby. I would love him and accept who he was no matter what was wrong.

One thing I realized was that Peter was narcissistic. He was overly indulged with himself. I could understand that aspect. I was so into myself, I didn't even want to have children. Whatever I wanted, I intended to get it, and I did. If I married, one had to marry me for me and not for what I could do for him.

So, I started paying close attention to Peter, and I noticed behaviors that were odd. But I would always reflect back to what one of my graduate professors said when I was in school at Georgia State University. He would tell us not to go home and start using our education on our family members. He would tell us not to be observing and analyzing everyone trying to label them as neurotic or psychotic.

We all moved in and out of neurosis as we handled difficult problems and situations. The difference between neurotics and psychotics is that in a neurotic state, one had a strong sense of reality. In dealing with and going through various challenges, one realized that they were temporal. People would get through them and snap back to their senses and understand that they'd handled the problems successfully.

On the other hand, a few of us may find ourselves all alone. It's like being on Chimney Rock looking down and out at others as if you had no clue of who you were, where you were, or what you were supposed to be doing. You had no grasp of the real world. You stayed out there on that rock for quite a long time . . . years. The length of time you stayed out there on that rock really helped the therapist to classify your behavior properly.

We all have things we have worked on. No one is perfect, and we all could use help in some area of our lives. For my Baby, it seemed the more issues that became apparent, the more it became clear why I was the partner and not someone else. I just loved on him and loved on him even more.

He needed me, and I gained a deep sense of purpose. I knew that no matter what it looked like to my family or others, I was truly doing what I was supposed to be doing right now. I actually became a gazing stock wherever we went because of his unusual behaviors. On a few occasions, I became a laughing stock. It was demeaning. Then, I had to come to the realization that this marriage was not about me. It was about my inward charge to be there for Peter, to help him, and to care for him. I was on a mission. When I thought about the things that made me feel so badly, those were moments in public places.

During those times of deep humiliation, I resorted to introspecting. I said to myself, "I know this isn't happening to me; not Toni Baldwin, who was the head majorette in her senior year at Dillard High School and who was the Alpha Sweetheart her senior year at Fayetteville State University. No, no, no, this was definitely not happening to Toni Baldwin." My ego was wounded. I was offended by his behavior.

Then, I would simply gain my composure and remind myself that this wasn't about me. But I must admit that I had to supplicate, send up timber to God as my maternal grandmother used to say. It was seriously hard, but I was determined to persevere. The Lord told me that I was equipped for the task and that it was by His authority and might that I would succeed. One thing I knew was that I needed to have my role defined. After really crying out to God, it became apparent that I was to operate in the role of caregiver rather than a spouse.

I was reminded of Proverb 27:7: *The full soul loatheth an honeycomb; but to the hungry soul, every bitter thing is sweet.* Truly, I was hungry. I needed clarity and understanding. The role of caretaker left a void that only God could fulfill.

"God, I need You, I really yearn for Your touch. My world was falling apart. It's You and You alone. My heart pantheth for you (Psalm 42:1). *Deep calleth unto deep at the noise of thy waterspouts; all thy waves and thy billows are gone over me* (Psalm 42:7). Yet I know, Lord, You will command Your loving kindness to shower me in the daytime (Psalm 42:8). In the night hours, Your song shall be with me." I got connected to God on a profound, intimate level. I refuse to damage my relationship with God. I am linked for life.

What complicated our lifestyle even more was when his joints and muscles started causing problems. He was swelling in his ankles and feet and his fingers started getting stiff. The eventual diagnosis was two kinds of arthritis: rheumatoid and osteoarthritis. My poor Baby. . . "What if I were in his shoes?" I would hope that God would put me in the hands of someone who would love, cherish, and take care of me.

God had chosen me for the task at hand. He formed me in my mother's womb for the task at hand. My temperance and my tolerance level were instilled in me for the task at hand. I waited on the Lord because of the waiting spirit inside of me. Psalm 139:16 says, *"Thine eyes did see my substance, yet being unperfect: and in thy book all my members were written, which in continuance were fashioned, when as yet there was none of them."*

I do not doubt for one minute that I was fulfilling the will of the Lord. He had enabled me to take care of my baby. One night I awoke three times. The first time was 1:10 a.m., and the second time was 3:30. I finally got up at 5:15 and waited on the Lord. I realized as Samuel did that that was unusual. I got up and sat on the side of the bed and that was when the Lord gave the Scriptural reference of Psalm 139. To take care of someone requires reaching out beyond who you are and just giving your all and all for the sake of that individual's well being.

Psalm 139:17 says, *"How precious also are thy thoughts unto me, O God! How great is the sum of them!"* What a great feeling to know that God trusted me in this situation. He knew that whatever He told me to do I would do. He knew the task was so important that it required immeasurable stamina and endurance. These are character traits He gave me. So, I was up for the task.

It was necessary for me to wrap my mind around the notion that God's thoughts of little ole me were so cherished by Him. God loved me. God adored me. God cherished me. Wow! How awesome was that. God counted on me. His thoughts were so great toward me. If I should count them, they would be more in number than the sand. . . I could handle taking care of my Baby.

Chapter Sixteen

Through It All

When I began to see real clues of the change in my Baby's mental capacity, it drew me even closer to him. Little things like taking a bath had changed. He was such a sharp dresser and so mindful of his appearance. It was very strange to walk by him and to detect an odor.

I started paying attention when he was bathing. In fact, I just went into the bathroom and sat down. He had forgotten how to take a bath. He would sit in the tub splashing the water over his body with the facial cloth. He would put soap on the cloth but not rub it on his body. I didn't see him touch his face or neck at all. I washed his back as I normally did when he finished bathing.

I realized that I had to start giving him a bath. I thought about taking showers together, which would be an easy way to get the job done. But I also considered the danger of falling. We weren't as agile as we used to be.

That brought to mind what one of the elders had said at a recent conference. He related that there are new categories of senior status now. In your sixties, you are "young old," and in your seventies, you are "middle old." Thus, in your eighties and nineties, you are just plain "old, old."

Since I was young old, I couldn't afford to take slippery chances. Plus, taking a bath was still a luxury. I enjoyed the feel of soaking my bottom and my feet. It made me feel cleaner than taking a shower.

I asked him if I could give him a bath, and he told me it was okay.

Another change was that I had to accompany him to the bathroom. It gradually progressed to setting up a bathroom schedule due to the fact that he would forget to go. With the help of disposable wipes, we were able to maintain good personal hygiene, especially in public facilities. Public restrooms caused problems. Here in America, we had made great strides in providing for the handicapped. There were bathrooms designed to accommodate wheelchairs for people who could go by themselves or with someone of the same gender. Unfortunately, there were no public bathrooms for males and females to use together.

When I would take Peter to the bathroom in churches, restaurants, and the mall, I had to go to the manager for assistance. The manager on duty would have to be sure that the bathroom was clear, so I could go in with my husband. That was usually the men's room, and the manager would hold the door or ask one of the waitresses to do so.

Our first encounter with this was at Elon University when my great niece graduated. I took him into the ladies' restroom, because the men's room was too far away. When everyone cleared out, we went in. More women came in after we were in the stall. We kept waiting to come out trying to wait for the ladies to leave. After several minutes, we just came on out. One woman dropped her lipstick into the sink. Another's hand flew to her chest. I said not one word. I assisted him with washing his hands and hoped they were intelligent enough to get the point. After all, we were on a college campus.

I took him with me so much that folk would ask me where he was when he was not with me. They would ask me where my other half was and would tell me how funny I looked without him. These were times when he was at the adult day care facility. They provided excellent care; however, there was neither overnight care nor weekend care.

It became evident that I needed assistance. I needed a certified nursing assistant. I learned they were called CNA's. I also needed a sitter when I had meetings to attend and he couldn't go. The CNA handled bathing, dressing, and feeding when I was gone. It got to the point where I needed assistance seven days a week.

There was something else that I had to get settled in my spirit—my husband's spiritual consciousness and awareness. I knew at first how he loved Jesus and how he loved going to Sunday School and church. That year we'd had a revival at our church, and I was amazed at how my baby was lifting his hands and praising the Lord during the message. It wasn't in response to a song. No, this was in response to the preacher. I was getting the impression that Peter was really connecting with the Word. There was such an anointing on him that night. It reminded me of the night that he prayed for my sister, Minnie, who was in a nursing home. He prayed out of his heart and after about an hour, he finished and was so weak from the anointing that was on him, he had to sit down.

So, during the revival, I got peace about the state of my husband's mind and the connection and relationship he had with the Father.

Chapter Seventeen

Birthing My Baby

It had been seven and a half years, and my Baby had finally been released physically from the unpredictable world in which we lived. He had been released into a State operated Veterans Nursing Home which was more akin to his own private world. He moved about freely without the danger of falling, because he resided now in a single-level home. He walked up to people and just stood there, and they didn't get offended. He rubbed on his legs and knees when he sat down, and people didn't look at him like he was strange. He explored and examined things without being chided. There were manipulatives on the walls and tables, and the residents handled them at will. If he didn't talk, he wasn't badgered about it. He was encouraged to participate in activities not forced or strongly driven. He was given choices that enhanced thinking capabilities, which, as we knew, were so limited.

Most of the time when I visited, there was a wonderful time of sharing. The activity director or one of the nurses would inform me that Peter had been dancing and having loads of fun. He laughed and did a lot of smiling. That made me feel good and at ease to hear from different people that he was doing fine. He was neither depressed nor lonely.

Peter could enjoy the activities, because his mind was still capable of comprehending what was going on around him. This was a very good thing. He was still ambulant, and that was truly a blessing. He loved to walk and he did so throughout the day, unless they were observing quiet time. In that case, they encouraged him to sit and relax.

The placement at this long-term care facility was well orchestrated by God. More than a year earlier, I was diagnosed with a goiter on my neck. I wanted it removed but was unable to schedule surgery until I found proper care for my husband. After having found a place, I had the surgery. During that time, my husband spent two weeks in respite care at the VAH while I recuperated from surgery. Prior to surgery, I had decided that it was time for him to be placed in long-term care. Consequently, the time had arrived for placement in the facility. So, he transitioned from respite care to the State Veterans Nursing Home.

The Lord arranged this placement. I'd found out about government and state nursing homes for veterans from an admissions officer at another nursing home. What I learned was that there are two types of veterans' homes, federal and state. For placement in the federal home, the illness had to be service connected. For placement in the state home, the illness did not have to be service connected. I was given the name and phone number of the director of admissions at the state operated home. That was the best news ever. The two facilities were adjacent to one another, and both were only five minutes from where we lived.

I immediately called the number and explained our situation to the admissions director. It was a Tuesday, and I was scheduled to pick Peter up on Thursday of that week. Things had to move hurriedly. The officer totally understood my concern about making the transition smooth and easy from temporary care to long-term care. She agreed to accept him with short notice as long as I had the FL-2 form along with the discharge papers from his primary care doctor. One thing that worked to our advantage was that he was already at the federal veterans home, so they knew he qualified for service.

I picked up another FL-2 form from the same lady, so I could have an extra form in case I needed another one if the first one got lost. I called the social worker at the VAH, and he told me he would see to it that the doctor got the form. I agreed to this; however, I still felt I needed to take one of the FL-2's that I had to the hospital to see if I could give it to the doctor myself. Somehow, I just felt I needed to do that.

It was very, very rare for a civilian to see a doctor without an appointment. But, with the form in my hand, I stepped into the elevator and at the first stop, guess who was standing there when the elevator door opened?

The doctor that I needed to see stepped into the elevator and said, "Hello there Mrs. Daniels, how is it going?"

"Hi Dr. Zeckulaw, you're the very person I came to see. I need you to complete this FL-2 application form in order to place my husband in the state operated veterans home. I need it today."

He assured me that it would be no problem. He was already aware of my decision, because I'd consulted him about it. So, Dr. Zeckulaw took the form and told me that he would give it to the social worker who would get it to the admissions director at the state facility.

On that Thursday morning, I went to pick up my husband. I needed to get him to the facility by 12:30 p.m. The admissions director told me that she had everything all set. The staff was informed, and his room was ready for his arrival. He had already eaten breakfast, so I took him to the TV room to wait on the doctor's discharge orders. This room was cozy. It was just enough privacy for two people about to make a move that would separate them. I needed that space. I reflected on the special moments we had together and wondered how we would make it apart from each other. About that time, I heard a voice say,

"Mrs. Daniels, how did everything go at the nursing home?"

I looked around and it was Dr. Zeckulaw.

"Hello Doc, my husband was accepted. Now, I need the discharge orders from you."

The doctor responded, "I didn't get the word. I will sit down and type them now. It won't take long. Had I known, they would have been ready. I apologize."

"Doc, if I had known to tell you directly, I would have. I thought the social worker would inform you."

"No, that was the responsibility of the family member."

"Dr. Zeckulaw, I apologize for dropping the ball. When the ball is in my court, I like to perform my duties well. I was not aware of that policy."

He understood and told me there was no problem and that he would have the orders ready soon.

The doctor came up for a staff briefing, but took time to complete the final papers for my husband's placement. It was the second divine intervention with this doctor. We made it to the facility somewhat behind schedule, but we made it. Through one's wildest imagination, those two contacts with Dr. Zeckulaw couldn't have been so strategically orchestrated. Our finite minds couldn't have arranged those encounters.

Chapter Eighteen

My Baby

It's a joy when you see someone operating in their own world and wanting to bring you in with them. Oftentimes, my Baby would motion for me to look at something and just start smiling and nodding his head. It could have been someone putting his fingers in his mouth as if he had just eaten some Kentucky Fried Chicken. It might even have been a noise somewhere in the room, and Peter would draw my attention to it. He was attentive to everything going on around him. He was okay with instant outbursts, loud commotions, and strange noises.

Sometimes he got up and walked over to others and stood there by their wheelchair or the person. Wasn't that a good lesson to learn? When others were in distress, someone being near was comforting enough without the individual having to converse verbally. It told the person, "I'm with you, and I feel you."

My husband was free to be himself. He didn't have to look around when he did something to see if he was meeting somebody's approval. He was happy, and it made me happy. I used to cry, agonizing over his condition. Now, I shed tears of joy. I made every attempt to see the world through his eyes. He loved to invite me in and would take me by the hand or beckon for me to follow him somewhere. I remember him taking me and just standing in the midst of a few patients. I gathered that it was his way of introducing me to them. So, I told them my name and chatted with them for a few minutes. It pleased him, because he starting nodding his head.

I was so thankful, because he was in an environment where he could be himself. He was talking a little bit, and I had to tune in very closely when we were together so that I didn't miss those rare occasions. They were phrases, not sentences. They usually related to something around him, on TV or in his mind. That was why I had to be emotionally connected when I visited. I didn't want to miss opportunities to explore his world with him.

I really felt that my husband had a renewed feeling of self-respect. When he was at home, it was a constant reminder of all the things he could no longer do. His favorite pastimes were bowling and playing golf. His sense of independence was lost when he could no longer drive. With the varied daily activities at the facility, his self-esteem was enhanced as well. It was a real boost to his ego when most of the day was spent meeting the approval of those around him and not being afraid of breaking rules.

At home, I was always seeing where he was and checking to be sure he was safe and not wandering outside or in a place where he was endangered, being sure that the car keys were out of sight. . . .

While I was trying to provide a safe and comfortable home environment, at times it was difficult for Peter to be at ease. Now, it was fascinating to know that all of it had changed. My Baby was so content now. The Scripture came to mind how David ascribes the awesomeness of God in Psalm 104 in regards to the clouds and the atmosphere. I thought about my Baby all the time and I sometimes would get the impression that he was in his world somewhere out there in the atmosphere maneuvering as if he was actually walking on the wings of the wind.

My Journey to Writing

I, Eugenia Antoinette Baldwin, was born in Goldsboro, North Carolina. My parents, Eugene and Ida Dorothy Baldwin, had two other children, Litha Almetria and Minnie Margorie. After our parents divorced, we were reared by our maternal grandmother, Minnie Best. Our mom remarried and we have eight other siblings, six brothers and two sisters. We spent lots of time at our mom's and even stayed overnight occasionally. Mother was definitely involved with our upbringing. She usually made the final decisions and was known to be a strict disciplinarian regarding school and social issues. Mother was very smart and she could figure things out before we even finished telling her what was on our mind. It was important to her that we expressed ourselves and we had ample opportunities as we sat at the dinner table after school sharing our daily activities.

On days that we were at home with our grandmother, Minnie, whom we affectionately called Ma Ment, we would still dine together after school expressing how our day had gone and being entertained by Ma Ment's humor. Aunt Juanita, whom we called Aunt Sissy, was Ma Ment's sister.

She prepared our daily meals because Ma Ment worked as a household technician which was referred to as a domestic worker or cook. Ma Ment was short in statue, loving and cuddly. I loved school and have always enjoyed learning. Through early childhood experiences, I discovered the importance of imparting my thoughts whether verbally or in written form. I was determined to make my voice heard.

A notable and very dreadful moment for me happened during my first year of school after having attended kindergarten. Kindergarten was not taught at the public schools at that time, at least where we lived. Kindergarten was taught at Faith Tabernacle by a member of my neighborhood church. Mother enrolled me in school in the first grade. After having been in school a couple of months, the principal told my teacher that I could not return to school. On that particular day, the teacher asked me to remain after school because she needed to speak to me. I was so happy because I felt she wanted me to do something special the next day in class. I was eager to hear what she had to say because I had already made up my mind to say yes. I perked up and was curiously anticipating the moment. The teacher began telling me what the principal had said. The sparkle in my eyes were replaced with tears. My shoulders dropped and my little voice just left me. I could not speak. I was so hurt and so upset. I really loved school. I didn't know what to do.

It took me forever to make it home that day. I went the long way home. Instead of taking the short cut by walking to the end of the school yard and jumping the "ditch," I walked that block very, very slowly. I could stand in the school yard and see my house because it was only one street over. Rather than getting home in five minutes, I got home in thirty minutes.

When I did get home that day, my mom, my grandmother, my aunt, and my sisters were there waiting for me. They could tell by my countenance that I knew about the bad news. I got the warmest "bear" hugs and "sweetest kisses" from my family. I found out that my cousin's mother had told the principal that I was only five years old, not six years old. My cousin's mother got caught and her daughter had to stay home from school and wait until the next year. So she let the cat out the bag on my mother. It turned out that my mom, like a few other moms, had changed my birthday on my birth certificate.

I blamed the principal for putting me out of school and it made me eager to return and to show all of them what a terrible mistake they had made by sending me home. I had something to prove and it instilled a drive in me to do my best, to speak up for myself, and to let folk know that I am in the room.

This is my first book and I am already working on my second one.

About the Author

Eugenia Daniels graduated from Dillard High School in Goldsboro, North Carolina and attended Fayetteville State University where she received a Bachelor of Science Degree in Business Education. She later earned a Master of Education Degree with a concentration in Counseling and Psychological Services from Georgia State University. Her professional career includes counseling, teaching at the high school and community college levels, and doing social work. She has traveled to several European countries including Germany, Holland, England and Spain. While in Germany, she directed the Army Education Center where she was employed as an Education Services Specialist.

She was called to preach over fifteen years ago. She founded Pait's Outreach Ministry for Children, Inc. Eugenia enjoys teaching the Word and organized a Senior Outreach Bible Study at Walnut Street School Apartments in Goldsboro. Her prayer is that the Lord will fulfill the secret petitions of her heart by opening doors in the Third World Countries for her to propagate the Gospel through mission and evangelism.

The author is available for book signings, workshops, seminars, retreats, or other speaking opportunities. Send an email to:

eugeniadaniels2@gmail.com

Join her on Twitter at:

http://www.twitter.com/toniment

Join her on Facebook at:

http://www.facebook.com/eugenia.daniels

For information on ordering copies of *My Poor Baby,* please contact the author or Kingdom Living Publishing:

Kingdom Living Publishing
P.O. Box 660
Accokeek, Maryland 20607
publish@kingdomlivingbooks.com
(301) 275-9014